Ermengarda Greville- Nugent

A Land of Mosques And Marabouts

Ermengarda Greville- Nugent

A Land of Mosques And Marabouts

ISBN/EAN: 9783744753142

Printed in Europe, USA, Canada, Australia, Japan

Cover: Foto ©Andreas Hilbeck / pixelio.de

More available books at **www.hansebooks.com**

A LAND OF MOSQUES

AND MARABOUTS

BY THE
HON. MRS. GREVILLE-NUGENT,
AUTHOR OF
"THE RUINS OF GOREN, AND OTHER POEMS."

WITH ILLUSTRATIONS.

LONDON: CHAPMAN & HALL, LD.
1894.

TO

MY HUSBAND,

THESE MEMORIES OF SOME HAPPY MONTHS

SPENT WITH HIM

IN THE COUNTRY OF THE MOORS

ARE DEDICATED.

ÉTOILES FILANTES.

Il fait nuit! Que c'est doux d'être assise
   À côté de toi, où les roses
Sur le balcon remuent dans la brise
   Leurs boutons parfumés et mi-closes.

Ayant toi, n'ais-je pas tout ce qu'il me faut
   Sous le ciel moins profond que tes yeux?
Ce beau ciel de l'Afrique, où là-haut
   Une étoile se détache de ses feux!

Comme la lame d'une glaive, sur le seuil
   Tremblant subitement, dans la voûte
Elle se jette—elle s'enfuit.—Aucun œil
   Saura suivre cet astre dans sa route.

Mais le ciel qui la voit parcourir
   Ainsi loin de son immense toile,
Ne perd jamais le doux souvenir
   Qui l'a laissé la précieuse étoile.

Ô toi, mon époux et mon roi,
   Chaque regard, chaque caresse attendrie,
Et tous tes baisers sont pour moi
   Les étoiles filantes de ma vie!

Alger. 1893.

CONTENTS.

ALGERIA.

CHAPTER I.

ALGIERS.

	PAGE
Algiers—Its past—How the dey used his fan, and what came of it—A view from the Place du Gouvernement—An outdoor aquarium—A farewell, a welcome, and a funeral—A dinner à l'Algerien—The Arab town by night ...	1

CHAPTER II.

ALGIERS.

The Arab town by day—The ghosts of the Kasbah—The "Pavilion of the Fan"—A maker of guitars—Moorish wares and their vendors—In a Café Maure—A dear old lady—"Eyes and no eyes"—The Jewish quarter—Examples of Moorish architecture—Old Salem the Soudanese—The Amiranté—The "Captives in Barbarie"—An Office for "Apostates to Turcism"—The end of the Algerine pirates   21

CHAPTER III.

ARABS "CHEZ EUX."

Their families and *fêtes*—Sidi Mustafa and his home—My first introduction to kouss-konss—A Moorish wedding feast—An Arab conjurer—The scorpion-eating Aïssouas—The Ouled-Naïls — The Lahabin-Bessiouf — The Negro dancers—Mahommed ben Hussein Cherif—Zorah—I study Arabian music under her auspices—An evening at the Marabout's—Mahommed ben Ahmed—Little Fatma 48

CHAPTER IV.

LEGENDS OF MOSQUES AND MARABOUTS.

The sacred buildings—The Mahommedan clergy—A religion of one belief and six duties—The zaouias—Legends of the mosques in Algiers—Legends of Sidi Abderrahman—The cadi and the slave—Legend of Sidi Bon-Gueddour—The story of the Marabout and the kahouaji—How to distinguish between a true Marabout and an impostor ... 75

CHAPTER V.

THE ENVIRONS OF ALGIERS.

Le Chateau d'H——.—The story of Ali Agha and the "Peeping Tom" of Birmandreis—The tombs at Bou-Zareah—A Kabyle village—The sands at Maddrab—The Corsairs' Creek—The "Fort des Revenants"—A soldier degraded—A modern mosque—The Algerian diligences—Hammam Melouan—Amongst the Kabyles of the Atlas Mountains ... 97

CHAPTER VI.

BLIDAH.

The orange groves—A Hammam—The fire-eaters—An Arab stud—The Gorges de la Chiffa and the Ruisseau des Singes—What France has done for Algeria 121

CONTENTS. xi

TUNISIA.

CHAPTER VII.

ON BOARD THE "ABD-EL-KAD'R."

Our voyage on board the *Abd-el-Kad'r*—Towns on the African coast—An Arab descendant of Saint Louis—Bizerta—A boys' school—A village of outcasts—Arrival at Tunis ... 132

CHAPTER VIII.

TUNIS.

An "arc de triomphe"—In the bazaars—The Dar-ed-Bey—The call to prayer—A caravanserai—The Street of Refuge—A Jewish wedding—A night stroll during Ramadan—The Café Maure 144

CHAPTER IX.

TUNIS.

The Bardo—A secret door—The Hall of Justice—An unlucky prophet—Palace of Kassar-Saïd—A state bed—The ruins of Carthage—A subterranean dwelling—The royal mausoleum—A perfumer's shop—A rich house in Tunis—The cadi's "divan"—*La mort sans phrase*—Envoi ... 159

APPENDIX 187

LIST OF ILLUSTRATIONS.

		PAGE
PORTRAITS (See page 37)	Frontispiece	
ALGIERS IN 1830	To face	8
A STREET IN THE ARAB QUARTER		35
COURT OF A HOUSE IN OLD ALGIERS ...		57
MOSQUE OF SIDI ABDERRAHMAN		90
ARAB GRAVES AT BOU-ZAREAH	,,	102
KABYLE VILLAGE ...		116
ARAB BOY AT WELL	,,	127
BOYS' SCHOOL AT BIZERTA ...	,,	138
TUNISIAN SOUKS	,,	146
THE CITY OF TUNIS		156
BEY'S BED, PALACE OF KASSAR-SAÏD ...	... ,,	167

A LAND OF MOSQUES AND MARABOUTS.

ALGERIA.

CHAPTER I.

ALGIERS.

Algiers—Its past—How the dey used his fan, and what came of it—A view from the Place du Gouvernement—An outdoor aquarium—A farewell, a welcome, and a funeral—A dinner à l'Algérien—The Arab town by night.

You who open this book, did you ever in childhood's story-devouring days read in tales of the fierce Corsairs of Barbary, or later, in the romantic years of youth, sigh for the Moors driven out from an ungrateful Spain? Have you ever felt a desire to know how it fares with their descendants in this year of grace? Do the thoughts of veiled houris, swathed in Oriental brocades and gauzes and tinkling with sequins, entice you to a nearer view? Would you penetrate beneath Moorish arches, smell the heavy attar of roses, and eat dates sweet as honey and fresh from the parent palm, while you watch the dancing of the Ouled-Naïls and listen to the hum of the derbouka?

Then, dear reader, fly with me in the travelling trunk of fancy, even as the Persian merchant we wot of did of old. Let us close the lid, pronounce the magic word, and soar over the chimney-tops of smoky London till we find ourselves far south where the skies are blue; amongst cities whose roofs are white and flat, broken here and there by a round cupola marking the grave of some Moslem saint, or a minaret whence the mueddin proclaims the " Allah il Allah." We will descend to ground here, if you please, and open the lid; and then, though I fear I cannot take you into the palace of a sultana such as our merchant had the good fortune to find, I can, if you will take my hand, lead you through these cities where the women walk veiled and trousered, where a strange monotonous music strikes the ear, and where a wealth of wondrously harmonized colour delights the eye. Pluck a few flowers with me from the soil of this marvellous Africa, that so, amid the mirk of dire December days in England, you may yet know that beauty and *la joie de vivre* are not yet wholly things of the past.

I fear I cannot lay claim to the laurels of an explorer in undiscovered fields—indeed, who can nowadays?—and possibly these lands may be already familiar to many of my readers who live in times when a ten-pound note apiece transports countless tourists every winter to Northern Africa. My only plea is a desire to give pleasure to those who have not been able to see for themselves, and *du reste* (to borrow a sentence from Mrs. Lynn Linton's beautiful essay on the "Bay of Naples") " An old thing filtered through a new medium sometimes puts on a new appearance, and my own keen appreciation of the beauty which was so fresh for me may perhaps give it a gloss of freshness for others."

My first impressions of Algiers—" El Djzaïr the beautiful "—were reaped, to be perfectly candid, in a downpour of rain! After spending one winter month there, one learns to say, like the Algerians, not " *il pleut,*" but " *il tombe de l'eau,*" for when it does rain it comes down in perfect waterspouts. But this is only during December, and without it the vines would be in a bad plight. Still, I own that to the enthusiastic traveller, full of expectations of hot sun, white mosques, palms, and bare-legged Arabs, it is a little discomposing to land from the steamer in a mackintosh, and to catch glimpses of mosque and palm trees both dripping wet. As for the sun, he was absent, and the bare-legged Arabs were represented by one, who, proudly pointing to a large copper badge on his arm, assured us in fluent French that we might with safety confide our *petits colis* to him, for was he not " Numero 1 de la Cie Transatlantique"? However, next morning the sun was at his post, and when emerging from the courtyard of the Hôtel de la Régence we found ourselves in the full glare of heat on the Place du Gouvernement, with Arabs galore, and vendors of violets and roses importuning us at every step, we felt that we had indeed left the land of fogs behind us.

The Place du Gouvernement is an historic site. What fights the rocks on which it stands must have witnessed, while the waves which lap them have been stained by the death-wounds of many races. For Algiers, this smiling semi-Arab, semi-French city, was once Icosium of the ancient world, founded, it is said, by twenty companions of Hercules; and Phœnicians, Romans, Berbers, and Byzantine Greeks have in succession conquered her. The Berbers, whose descendants, the Kabyles, are spread over Algeria to this day, still retaining their separate language, called her Mezarhanna. Then came the Arabs who, early in the eighth century, invaded

Africa, led by that grand old saint and warrior, Sidi Okba, who subdued city after city and province after province to Islam, and who, after penetrating to the extremity of Morocco, knelt down on the sea-shore and exclaimed, "Oh that there were yet more lands left for me to conquer in the name of the Prophet!" Poor Sidi Okba! He was killed while battling with a revolted tribe at last, and lies buried in the oldest mosque in Africa, in the town called by his name, near Biskra at the mouth of the Great Desert. Then, later on, when those of his followers who had crossed to Spain and settled there, were finally expulsed, what could they do but seek again the African shores which their forefathers had quitted? So they took shelter in all the towns along the coast from Tangier to Tunis; and here in Algiers they built these lovely houses with their courts and fountains which we will visit later. But inland they did not penetrate, leaving that to their wilder brethren the Arabs (properly so called), those Bedawin tribes who live in tents, for in Andalusia the Moors had learnt to love luxury and the life of cities. Then they commenced a continual harrying of the Spanish sea-board, avenging themselves for the loss of Granada by raids, in which they carried off numberless unhappy slaves, till, in 1509-10, Ferdinand the Catholic sent an expedition under

Cardinal Ximenes and Don Pedro Navarro, who took Oran and other towns and captured a little islet in the harbour of Algiers, whereon they erected the fort still known as the Pénon. Then comes the last act but one in this curious drama. The Algerine Moors, feeling anxious at the continual fire kept up by the Spaniards from this island-fortress, called in the aid of their fellow-believers the Turks, who in 1515 sent a fleet under Oroudj Barbarossa and his brother Khair-ed-din, and these terrific warriors routed the enemy. But the Turks, who had come to help, stayed to conquer. The Arab sheikh, who was then governor of Algiers, was treacherously slain, and in 1519 Khair-ed-din, who received at Constantinople the title of Capudan Pacha, was appointed by the sultan the first dey; this new possession being formally annexed as a part of the great Ottoman Empire, and thenceforward re-named "El Djzaïr." *

Thus they remained till 1830, cruelly and oppressively lording it over Moors and Arabs alike, who dared not say them nay, for was it not all done in the name of the Prophet and of his representative the Commander of the Faithful? They kept

* *i.e.* "The islands," from the numerous small islets in the harbour, which are now, however, connected with the mainland. From hence come the Spanish, French, and English corruptions, Argel, Alger, and Algiers.

up the old piratical traditions, too, and Algiers remained till late in the last century the terror of Christendom and the scourge of the seas.

But in 1830 the dey did a stupid thing. He lost his temper—always a fatal act—while sitting in his pavilion up in the Kasbah, one hot day, and struck the French consul, to whom he was giving audience, a blow on the cheek with his fan. Could Gallic blood stand such an insult? Never! *L'honneur de la patrie, la gloire de la France* must be vindicated! The consul withdrew from the august presence vowing vengeance, and sought redress from his sovereign; with the result that in the following year the French troops, effecting a landing at Sidi Ferruch, descended upon the town, and successfully bombarded the Kasbah, "till the gunpowder ran out at the heels of their boots." Thus fell proud Algiers after centuries of defiance. The Arabs collapsed and submitted, the Turkish janissaries and officials fled to Constantinople, and the Great Panjandrum himself, whose irascibility had brought about the whole disaster, abdicated and retired in disgrace to Europe.

In the accompanying illustration, taken from an old print of "La Place du Gouvernement en 1830," we see that the mosque "Djemâa el Djedid" stands on uneven rocks which slope down to the sea.

Adjoining it is a rampart through which cannons poke their nozzles, and in the foreground a soldier in the French uniform of that day keeps guard, with pyramids of round shot piled up suggestively to right and left of him. Now they have blasted the rocks and built *rampes* and steps down to the quay, and levelled and asphalted the large square space round the mosque. And they have beaten their swords into ploughshares, or, in other words, melted down the old Turkish guns and cast therefrom a " pleasing " equestrian statue by Marochetti of his Royal Highness the Duc d'Orleans, first Governor-General of Algeria, in 1830; which, wonderful to relate, has been allowed to stand through two revolutions. And this brings us back to the Place du Gouvernement, where, at the foot of the above-mentioned statue, we find ourselves after a long digression, which I trust the reader will pardon, or at any rate skip, should history bore him.

Take a seat on this bench with me, and watch the shifting kaleidoscope of faces and costumes, which to an artistic eye are an endless feast. Here comes a stately Arab, with his womenfolk behind him. He must be rich, for round his turban are wound many yards of camel's-hair wool, and under his burnous you catch glimpses of a kaftan of

ALGIERS IN 1830.

a glorious soft grass-green hue. The ladies, of course, are shrouded from head to foot in their white haïcks; their enormous baggy white trousers are gathered in round their ankles, hiding the shorter indoor pair which reach only to mid-leg. One slender hand holds the face-veil in its place, but you meet the glances of their flashing black eyes as they pass you. This man coming along now must be the cadi, or else some holy pilgrim, for all who meet him kiss his hand with veneration. Here is a coal-black Mozabite, and here a water-carrier from Biskra, with his picturesque copper jar on his shoulder. Here be Spaniards and Maltese and Italians (fishermen, mostly, and carters), and a Jewess in the *not* beautiful costume of the Algerian Juiverie. (We shall see the Tunisian Jewesses later on, all glittering with gold embroidery.) Here they wear ordinary European skirts, surmounted by a sort of "Zouave" and covered with a Paisley shawl; but by their heads ye shall know them, for their skulls are tightly swathed in a black silk covering drawn down as low as the forehead, to which at the back of the head is affixed a scarf of some bright-hued gauzy material. As for the he-Jews, they wear a fez with a dark blue turban rolled round it, dark caftans (some few retain the gaberdine), the usual baggy Moorish breeches coming to the knee, grey-blue woollen stockings, and high shoes covering the foot instead of the low open ones into which the Musulmans merely thrust their feet, and which can be evacuated at a moment's notice by their occupiers when the owner of the said feet has occasion to enter a house or mosque.

The principal door of the great mosque on our left stands in a steep street leading to the " Pêcheries," or fish-market, which latter is as good as an aquarium any day, for here indeed the saying " All's fish that comes to their net " is true, and a more extraordinary collection of marine monsters was never seen. Sea-serpents (apparently) of varying lengths, sea-urchins green and thorny, exquisite fishes of a rosy colour merging into scarlet like the hues of sunset, silvery *pageots*, queer crustaceans, octopuses, *loups de mer*, *chiens de mer*, and other mysterious creatures of the Mediterranean for whom it would be difficult to find English names. Not one of these are disdained by the Algerian fishermen and housewives, and what the rest of the community reject as useless, the Jews will haggle for and eat! Outside this building and all the way up to the mosque door are little stalls, the owners of which sit smilingly chattering under their coloured awning; stalls for shell-fish and bait; stalls, too, where the weird fishes of the Mediterranean are rivalled by still weirder fruits from the shores of Barbary. There are luscious *plaquemines* (globes of red-gold, like the apples of the Hesperides filled inside with the most delicious jelly), prickly *figues de Barbarie*, dates, and wild pineapples. Here, too, is a restaurant where you may déjeuner on the most delicious oysters at seventy-five centimes a dozen, and—let me whisper it—*bouille-à-baisse*; on *moules à la marinière*, with a *biftek* and very fair wine of mine host's own growing, all for an absurdly small sum; while you watch the mingled crowd of Spaniards in their red sashes, Arabs emerging from the mosque, laden donkeys, beggars in picturesque rags, and sellers of live-stock. These last are hawking Barbary apes—our poor little cousins whose wistful faces seem to say, "Do take us out of these cramped cages;" tortoises caught in the vineyards, of whose shells the Arabs fashion guitars; and exquisite green parrots. The whole scene makes a jumble of life and colour most characteristic of Algiers, and a perfect subject for a painter.

The Place du Gouvernement and the Boulevard de la République are the stages whereon most of the dramas of life in modern Algiers are played. I have seen a retiring general who had given in his *démission* hold his farewell parade there, embarking subsequently from the quay below, while the band of the Zouaves discoursed sad music, and the entire population bent their gaze on the out-gliding steamer. Even the waiters had run across from the opposite café, their napkins thrown over their heads; and the whole crowd, stirred by *un spectacle si émotionnant*, were holding alternately handkerchiefs and opera-glasses to their eyes. I have seen his successor welcomed by the fickle French populace a few short weeks later, with full honours of bunting and salutes, the Zouaves playing merrier strains this time, all the world in great gala, and a general air of "*Le roi est mort, vive le roi*" pervading everything. I have seen—a never-to-be-forgotten sight—the funeral cortège of that great and good man Cardinal Lavigerie; his body followed by men of all classes, civil and military, secular and religious. Bishops in violet copes, judges in scarlet and ermine, judges of the Court of Appeal in yellow robes and yellow capes, *avocats* in black gowns and bands; generals, admirals, mounted "Spahis" in turban and high red boots; the Chasseurs d'Afrique on their long-tailed Arab steeds; and the "Pères Blancs," that noble missionary order founded by the dead cardinal for work in Northern Africa, clad in their habit of white burnous and red fez, in which surely never Christian monk was seen before! To the

"Marche Funèbre" of Chopin they bore him down from the cathedral to the quay, where, amid the dull boom of cannon, the sable barge of state which received him was finally placed on board the steamer moored in readiness to take him to his last resting-place in Carthage.

But to-day all is smiling. The shops in the Bab-el-Oued and the Bab-Azoun are smartly decked; the mandoline players are tinkling away amongst the little outdoor tables of the Café Apollon; the golden date-sticks quiver on the palm trees; the flower stalls beneath them give forth sweetness; the toilettes are ravishing; and the square looks as gay as a little bit of Nice. Indeed, I have never been able to understand why the English birds of passage, instead of staying "*dans le mouvement*" in the town at such hotels as the Régence or the Oasis, should bury themselves sadly in the Anglo-Swiss pensions up on Mustapha Supérieur. There you may see them, a colony apart, walking primly in those sailor-hats and stiffly cut gowns, which are at once the amazement and amusement of French *élégantes;* and surrounded by their English chemist, their English library, and their English tradesman, who accommodates them with English cakes and cheeses, with "sittings" at the Presbyterian *temple*, and with villas at six thousand francs per season. Well, every one to his taste! But I doubt whether the invalids for whom their doctor has probably prescribed "change of scene" as well as "change of air," will get much of it under these circumstances, or ever see more of Moorish life and local colour than may be gained from meeting a passing donkey-driver on those "superior" heights.

Down here, however, the amount of local colour is almost bewildering to a new-comer; and our first dinner at a café on the gaslit Boulevard was something on this wise:—

SCENE.—*Table outside the Café de* ——.

Enter MONSIEUR *et* MADAME (*newly arrived*) *endeavouring to dine.*

1st Course.

MONSIEUR (*studying the "Carte du Vin"*).—"Comment! 'Metidjah,' 'Staoueli,' 'Tizi-Ouzou,' 'Bou-Medfa.' What, in the name of Bacchus, are these extraordinary beverages? Dites-donc, garçon, faites venir le maitre d'hôtel."

EXPLANATORY HEAD-WAITER (*politely*).—"Monsieur, ce sont les vins de l'Algerie, et j'espère que monsieur et madame les trouveront aussi bons que les vins de France."

MONSIEUR *and* MADAME *order, doubtfully, the wine with the least unpronounceable name.*

Enter ITINERANT NEWSVENDOR.—"V'la le *P'tit Journal*, cinq centimes, vient d'arriver de Marseilles."

MONSIEUR (*affably*).—"Merci, non."

Enter First Dog (*mixture of poodle and dachshund*), *on whom* MADAME *bestows a piece of bouilli from her "Petite Marmite" soup.*

Enter Second Dog (*chiefly bull-terrier, various other breeds thrown in*), *who endeavours to possess himself of the above bit. Difference of opinion, and exeunt both dogs.*

2nd Course. Fish (species unknown), *au beurre noir.*

MADAME.—"What an extraordinary looking fish! What is it called?"

E. H. W. (*urbanely*).—"Madame, c'est une espèce de poisson qu'on attrappe içi à Alger; mais je ne saurai vous dire son nom!"

Enter ARAB, *selling Kairouan carpets (made in Lyons).*—"Veux-tu des tapis Arabes?"*

MONSIEUR (*less affably*).—"Mais jamais de la vie!"

Enter RETURNING NEWSVENDOR.—"D'mandez *L'Algérien, Le Sport d'Alger, La Lanterne.*"

MADAME (*impatiently*).—"Non merci. Mais c'est inouï!"

3rd Course. *Becassines sur Croûtes.*

MONSIEUR (*angrily, after cautious sniff*).—"Sapristi, mais c'est un peu fort! Voilà que vous me flanquez là des becassines qui sont complètement faisandées."

E. H. W. (*always urbanely*).—"Monsieur, c'est que le gibier du pays n'est plus la même chose içi qu'en France. Les Arabes l'attrapent à trois jours d'ici dans l'intérieur, d'où ils l'apportent eux-mêmes à pied. Si monsieur désirait autre chose——?"

Enter ARAB, *selling native jewellery (just imported).* A. (*in broken French*).—"Bijoux Kabyles, anciens!"

MONSIEUR.—"Voyons ça! Mais c'est fait à Paris tout cela! Vieux blagueur, va!"

NEWSVENDOR (*returning*).—"V'la le *Gil Blas illustré, La Revue Algérienne*——"

MONSIEUR (*threateningly*).—"Puisque je vous ai déjà dit——!"

Enter INDIAN (*with tray*).—"You like see Benares work? I got very good shop here. I got shop Cairo. I sell Gibraltar; I sell Malta, too."

MONSIEUR (*jocularly*).—"I'll take care you don't 'sell' me!"

Enter ARAB *with antique swords (made yesterday).*

MONSIEUR.—"Veux-tu t'en aller? Cré nom d'un chien!"

Enter ARAB YOUTH *with blacking brushes.*—"Cirage, monsieur?"

MONSIEUR (*sarcastically*).—"B'en merci, surtout quand je porte des souliers en cuir jaune!"

Enter ARAB, *selling pipes;* ARAB, *selling purses;* ARAB, *selling coffee-cups, trays, and key-rings. Everybody selling something.*

MONSIEUR *and* MADAME (*with exasperation*).—". . .!"

---

* N.B.—In Arabic, *tutoiement* is the only form of addressing any one. Many Arabs, consequently, translating literally into French, adhere to the custom in that language also.

HEAD-WAITER (*soothingly*).—" Faut pas y faire attention, monsieur ! Moi, je ne m'en fiche pas mal de ces s——s indigènes !" (*To crowd, collectively*) " Allez-vous en au diable ! "

Vendors disperse tumultuously.

MONSIEUR *and* MADAME *proceed to order coffee (called in Algiers "* Nosi-bee " *and cognac (otherwise known there as "* Fine Métidja *").*

SCENE CLOSES.

All the same, you can dine exceedingly well in Algiers when once you have learnt not to order the fish or game of the country, and not to take the slightest notice of the Arab pedlars who persistently circle round your table.

" But where do they live, these *indigènes?* " you ask. Up in the old Moorish town, dear reader, where we will now proceed. For Algiers is, like a Neapolitan ice, in three layers. First you have the modern French part, representing the strawberry; then comes the Quartier Juif, which stands for the vanille; and beyond that the Arab town, which brings us finally to the pistache.

We will turn aside, then, from the lights and noise, and mount up these side streets by the Rue de la Lyre, and behold ! a change has come over the scene, and Time has stood still for centuries. There is no gate here, as at Tunis, to shut out the unbelievers; a sudden turn, and we are in it, " fairly in it." This contrast, so sudden, so bizarre, and by which you leap at one bound from the glaring arcades of the Rue de Rivoli (as it were) to the mysterious byways of the "Arabian Nights," forms one of the great charms of Algiers. Even the names of the streets have changed; and whereas five minutes ago you were strolling through the "Rue de la Liberté," or the "Place Malakoff," *now* you find yourself in the streets " of the Druses," " of the Red Sea," " of the Saracens," " of the Camel," " of the Janissaries," " of the Crescent," or " of Granada."

Narrow streets they are, in many places little more than gutters, mounting, ever mounting; houses all but touching overhead, with just room for a ray of moonlight here and there. The outer walls, looking on the streets, are broken only by a door, which is usually decorated with the hand of Fatma, surrounded by an arch carved in conventional designs, and protected by a porch made of green tiles, supported on wooden props. Here and there at irregular distances are tiny little casements, strongly barred, some not more than a foot long. The outjutting upper story is upheld by rough wooden poles, and the whole structure is covered with thick coats of whitewash. Little would any passer-by suspect the existence of the spacious inner courts, with their tiles of exquisite colour, their twisted columns, and their balustraded galleries, to

c

which those forbidding-looking portals would admit us if we only dared to push them aside.

It is December, but the air is hot and balmy, like a July evening in England, and the bright moon guides us, with sometimes an aiding lamp fixed in the wall. Round the corner comes the sound of tom-toms and derboukas from a house whose owner is giving a feast on some family occasion. Here a door opens, and some swarthy negro emerges, or bronzed Biskri, singing a strain of the curious Arabic music which it is so hard to imitate or describe. There a lover lurks beneath the shadow of a wall, gazing longingly at the house which shelters his adored one. And everywhere one *feels*, though one cannot see, that bright eyes are looking out at us through the iron bars of the tiny *mousherarbiyah* windows, their owners trying to catch glimpses (poor souls!) of the world they may never mix with openly. In the *kahouai* (Cafés Maures) you see mine host, the *kahouaji*, busily bending over the curious tiled structure which constitutes his *four économique;* while on benches within or grouped round the door lie his clients, smoking their long pipes, and listening, perhaps, to a professional *raconteur*, who is telling them those endless tales of which the East holds such inexhaustible stores.

The bazaars and stalls are mostly empty now, for

it is late; but here, by good luck, lingers one embroiderer, who is working "after hours" by the light of a candle to finish a bit of gold ornamentation for a woman's vest. And very beautiful work he turns out with those deft fingers as he sits cross-legged in his little den, only raised by one step from the street; work that would put to shame the productions of the "art needlework" establishments in London. He will sell you some of his gold thread, too, if you embroider yourself; weighing it before you in the scales, and burning the end of it in his candle to show you that it is genuine gold, which the flame will scorch but cannot blacken. (I wonder whether the marvellous freshness of the gold and silver threads, which one finds as bright as ever in sixteenth-century Spanish embroidery, is due to some secret of preparation left to the mediæval Spaniards from the time when the Moors were their masters?)

But our climb has been a long one, and here we are at the foot of the Kasbah, looking down over the steep declivity on which the city rests; looking down over cupolas, minarets, and flat-roofed houses, sheer down to the beautiful silver bay, with the shadowy Atlas Mountains beyond it. I think you will agree with me that one's first bird's-eye view of an African town is not a disappointing one.

We had better descend now, however; for, though the French police patrol constantly, it is wiser not to linger here too late without a native guide. Not that there is any danger from the Arabs themselves, but that there are many bad characters among the low Spaniards and Maltese who frequently take up their abode in this quarter, and who are handy with their knives on occasion.

To-morrow morning we will revisit the Moorish town by daylight, escaping from the noontide sunshine into these dark vaults and turnings. Picturesque and beautiful it must always be, and ever-varying in its different aspects. But to us, who still feel in imagination the hot breath of that balmy night, who mount the steep ways like walkers in their sleep, meeting sights which—whether faces, dresses, or buildings—seem all too strange, too beautiful, too impossible to be seen with waking eyes;—to us this first moonlight glimpse will remain for ever a thing apart in our souls; a jewel in that casket of memory wherein the most beautiful moments of our lives lay set and shrined, to be gazed on rarely, lest in the rude light of day they grow dim and vanish like fairy-gold.

CHAPTER II.

ALGIERS.

The Arab town by day—The ghosts of the Kasbah—The "Pavilion of the Fan"—A maker of guitars—Moorish wares and their vendors—In a Café Maure—A dear old lady—"Eyes and no eyes"—The Jewish quarter—Examples of Moorish architecture—Old Salem the Soudanese—The Amiranté—The "Captives in Barbarie"—An Office for "Apostates to Turcism"—The end of the Algerine pirates.

THE Kasbah (or fortress), built in 1516, stands here, as in every Moorish city, on the highest ground, frowning down like a grim sovereign on the houses, which cower, as subjects might, beneath its gaze.

It covers a vast area, intersected by the road now, but once completely enclosed by those huge walls over eight feet in thickness, of which part remain. Within their encircling arms stood a range of buildings which served as fortress, arsenal, court of justice, state prison,* the dey's palace, his mosque,

---

* Mr. Stanley Lane-Poole, in "The Barbary Corsairs," pp. 211-216, tells a sad story of four knights of Malta who were captured and imprisoned in this Kasbah. For eight years they were made to drag trucks of stone. "Once they formed a strange and sad feature in the

Turkish bath and harem; the whole being interspersed with gardens, of which now not a trace is left.

Across the painted door of the great entrance is stretched, idly enough now, an old and rusty chain. But look well at its motionless festoons, for on that chain have hung the hopes of many a condemned man—malefactor, escaped galley-slave, or what you will—who, could he only reach and touch it in time, was delivered from justice. I wonder how many did reach it? Fancy the wretched fugitive panting up the steep hill, his caftan flying, his brow streaming, as he steals an agonized backward glance at the cruel janissaries, who pursue him with their glittering scimetars drawn. Will he ever reach the summit in time? Will he, even then, be able to cross the level space that stretches beyond it? Will he after all have strength and breath left for a final spring to catch the scornful mocking chain that hangs so high up on that pitiless portal, before he falls down fainting in the scorching sun, stricken, but saved? That immense door never opened save to the dey himself. Perhaps the last dey may

wedding festivities of the [French] consul [which they were allowed to attend], when they assumed their perukes and court-dresses for the nonce, only to exchange them again for the badge of servitude when the joyful moment of liberty was over." They were ultimately ransomed.

have passed through it at his flight; but now the great bolts are drawn, and it will probably never again turn on its hinges; while the saving chain is no longer clutched at by breathless refugees. Passing within the walls one finds the remains of exquisite fountains, over which bright flowers may have trailed once; the buildings of the harem are supported on richly carved and twisted columns; the little mosque where the potentate went in state, surrounded by his courtiers, to invoke the aid of Allah has a graceful minaret enriched with fantastic tiles; and beyond it lies the bath where doubtless the tyrant, freeing himself from state cares for some hours in the heat of the day, came to dally with his houris.

Do you ever see ghosts? Then look now, for here come great black eunuchs going before to clear the way that no man-at-arms may loiter near with profane gaze. And see! the veiled ladies sweep down from the harem to the bath—Ayesha, Zuleika, Zorah, and the rest, with the slaves and odalisques. You can hear their sequins and their anklets clinking gently; their jewelled brocades leave behind them a lingering breath of musk and attar of roses.

Oh yes! there are many daylight ghosts in the Kasbah—ghosts of savage soldiery, of fanatic imams, ghosts of poor Christian slaves, too, beheaded here. They hung the heads up in a row in the dey's hall of audience, and when they were taken down the Turkish soldiers used to play at ball with the poor things, whose eyes were still wide open in a ghastly stare. Pah! it makes one creep to think of it all.

Standing in lonely state is one tall tower. It may have been a watch-tower, where Bluebeard looked out for his enemies; or it may have been used by the mueddin to call to prayer, for the minaret of the mosque is not a lofty one. Crossing the patio, we ascend by a staircase to the dey's private apartments, and there, projecting from the gallery over the courtyard, is the small wooden structure known now as the *pavilion de l'éventail*, where the last dey forgot his manners in the regrettable way described in the previous chapter. Who amongst the crowd of trembling sycophants surrounding his divan could have foreseen that the hours of his tyranny were even then numbered, and that on that very day was to occur the "episode of the fan," which, as that implement came in contact with the cheek of M. le Consul Français, was destined to cause their master's downfall?

Passing through a small door, we emerge on to the "terrace" (or flat roof-walk so called in Moorish houses, answering in English to the "leads"), from whence can be surveyed a very large slice of Algeria. Yonder is the whole grand sweep of the bay, the slopes of Bou-Zareah and Birmandreis, studded with white houses and cupolas. There are the two great Christian basilicas of Notre Dame d'Afrique on one side of us, and of the Koubba on the other, each built on a height overlooking the sea, each recalling somewhat in their domed outlines the style of a mosque, yet each proclaiming proudly the triumph of Christ over Islam. At our feet lies Algiers with its suburbs of St. Eugène, Agha, and Mustapha; below the latter stretch the Champ de Manœuvres and the Oasis of Ste. Marie, with its shady expanse of palms and bananas. In this clear atmosphere you can trace the outline of the bay right away to Cap Matifou, and beyond it is the wild country of the Kabyles, crowned by the stately Atlas range.

The Kasbah is now completely given up to the accommodation of the artillery, whose barracks are there, and an order to visit it must be obtained from the commandant. Even then very little is actually shown, as the interiors of the mosque and tower are converted into magazines, canteens, etc., the harem and other buildings into the men's *caserne*, and the dey's dwelling into officers' quarters. We luckily had a friend at court, however, in the shape of an officer of the reserve; so we selected the time when he was " making his twenty-eight days" of service, for our visit. He was of course able to take us through the officers' rooms, not accessible to the public, where many an exquisite painted ceiling, tiled panel, or stuccoed wall remain to tell of former splendour. Being allowed to "prowl" on my own account, I came suddenly upon a little neglected tiled oven, such as may still be seen in every Café Maure, and which must have been used for the dey himself, for it stood in an anteroom just off his own apartments; and I wondered if any much-harassed slave ever tried to mix a little poison with his Sublimity's coffee. Probably it was so, for few of these personages died natural deaths.

The deys—who were at first chosen by the Porte—had of course other palaces besides the Kasbah, such as the Djenana, or Palace of Gardens (now demolished), and others. But a century after the Turkish conquest the janissaries got permission to select their dey for themselves (a foreshadowing of Home Rule, in fact), his election being then confirmed by the Imperial firman, as a mere matter of form. The power thus vested in the janissaries at once led to violent factions; the deys were frequently murdered to make room for some popular favourite, and no doubt became gradually glad to avail themselves of this stronghold as their residence. The notorious Ali (the last but one) fled there in 1817, after a revolt occasioned by his cruelty; and Hussein Pacha, the last dey, is said to have quitted it only twice during his reign. The French on entering the place found a vast treasure concealed there.

Across the road, and outside the walls, stands the little church of Ste. Croix, formerly a mosque; the columns inside remain intact, but the octagonal-shaped minaret now supports the Cross instead of the Crescent. I could not help smiling at an incident which occurred on my first visit to this church. Two Arabs, from curiosity, had followed us in from the road, and I heard one explaining to the other that the holy water stoup was for the Christians to wash their hands in before service! No doubt he had some hazy idea that we, like them, must go through specified ablutions in connection with public worship. I did not think it worth while to undeceive them verbally, for Arabs, as a rule, are pigheaded in regard to their opinions; but on leaving I ostentatiously made the sign of the cross with the holy water, so that they might draw their own deductions.

We turn down into the town here—where you will—diving into the curious streets, dark and cool and mysterious even at noonday. Oh, those delicious windings and *impasses* of a Moorish town! who can describe their charm? How on earth the inhabitants of this rabbit-warren ever find their own particular nests again I have never been able to understand. One hardly ever "happens" upon the same street twice in one's ramblings; and, though the French municipality have thoughtfully stuck up neat blue enamel labels at every corner, they have only succeeded in giving a tiresome touch of civilization which breaks the charm, cannot be required by the Moors, who for centuries found their way without them, and does not materially assist the stranger where the turns and twists are so labyrinthine.

One of the most remarkable features about this quarter is its silence, which forms a curious contrast to the animated roar in the Tunisian *souks*. Here everybody seems asleep or spell-struck. Nor are there any regular bazaars, as in most Moslem towns; only here and there, among the houses, are little dens in which one or more workers are gently plying their various trades. They are not in any hurry, apparently; nor do they dream of inviting you to buy their wares.

Here is a tall, handsome young Moor, who is fashioning the quaint little two-stringed guitars on which his kind thrum in the idle evening hours. Overhead you may see finished ones of varying sorts and sizes hanging up. There are those made of tortoiseshell, for instance, and their construction is of the simplest. You merely cover the hollow side of the shell with a thin piece of wood, thrust one end of a stick about a foot and a half long into the shell, transfix the said stick with rudely finished heads at the other end, string it with two strands of catgut passed over a little wooden "bridge," and there you are! These little guitars vary according to the size of the shell, but the tortoises are rarely more than six or seven inches long. Again, there is a smarter kind, made of wood, covered with red or green velvet, studded with cowrie-shells, and with sometimes a small looking-glass inserted. On the reverse side is a parchment face, generally decorated with painted designs, and this instrument is also two-stringed. None of them cost more than two or three francs, and they make a pleasant little *pizzicato* accompaniment to the weird "songs of Araby." Then we come to a sweetmeat stall with wondrous creations in the lollipop line; and here is a deep den from whose darkling recesses come gleams of cloth of gold and rose-coloured brocade to fashion the women's vests and trousers withal. Next to it is a bookshop, having its shelves piled with Arabic romances and cunningly printed mottoes from the Korán on green or crimson grounds, which the faithful frame and hang up on their walls, and which are not so very far removed in idea, after all, from the "illuminated texts" sometimes seen in old-fashioned English bedrooms. Here sits cross-legged a maker of burnouses working a little ornamentation in green silk round the neck of an almost completed one. Anon some tall and bronzed son of the desert will purchase it, and, wrapping it in stately folds round his majestic form, will stalk away in it to a marriage-feast perhaps. In front of a stall stocked with queer-looking cheeses and such-like commodities, stands its M'zabite keeper, black as coal. A few old women, veiled and shrouded as carefully as though they were still young and fair, are chaffering over the goods displayed there. A string of donkeys—those pretty Arab donkeys with their coats in splendid condition, and their dear little fluffy faces—force us against the wall to make room for them and their paniers. And now a brawny, bare-legged seller of oranges goes down with his basket poised on his head towards the lower town, where you may meet him again hawking his wares with the monotonous cry of "Des Mandarines," or "El China" (as the Arabs call the fruit, since orange-trees were imported from China).

Here is a Café Maure, or *kahoua*. I cannot recommend the coffee they give you there; but we will enter, for the sake of studying the *habitués*. Some are deep in a game of "damma" (their form of draughts) on rude boards with the squares hollowed out. Others are playing cards—they are inveterate gamblers—for cups of coffee; others taking their siesta at full length on the benches with their faces covered by the burnous, and one is singing snatches of a wild song. Over all is the réposeful solemnity of the East, so different from the cackling unrest of a café full of Europeans. They do not rise as the ladies of the party enter, for women, to their ideas, are slaves on whom such marks of deference would be quite thrown away; but in response to our general greeting of "*Es-salaam alikoum*" ("Peace be unto you"), they will respond, "*Oua alikoum es-salaam*" ("And on you peace"); unless, indeed, seeing we be mere Christians, they may cut down the formula to "*Oua alikoum*" ("And on you"), for this "peace" is the peace of Paradise, bestowed only on true believers, and should never be spoken of save between Musulman and Musulman. To a mixed gathering, including those of their own faith as well as Jews and Christians, they will say, "*Es-salaam ala men ettebaa el houda*" ("Peace be on him who follows the right way"), by this means avoiding the direct salutation of Christian or Jew.

The kahoua is barely furnished, only a few

benches and a table or two besides the tiled stove. On the walls you will probably find a quaint old drawing—half map, half picture—of the Holy City of Mecca; or of a fleet of mediæval ships ploughing their way through conventional waves, with doubtless a convoy of pilgrims on board; and everywhere those texts from the Korán, in ornamental writing, so interwoven and contorted that often the most learned Arabs cannot themselves decipher it.

"*Iā kahowaji*," you call, "*aitini kahoua*" ("Oh, seller of coffee, give me coffee"), adding, if your tastes coincide with those of your humble servant, "*Kahoua mouz, machi halona*" ("Café Turque, not the ordinary kind"). It comes in queer little oval cups with no handles, standing in outer bowls shaped like egg-cups, and made ordinarily of hammered brass or other common metal, but in rich men's palaces of the finest gold and silver filagree inlaid with coral and studded with turquoise. Here, in Algiers, they have become too much contaminated by intercourse with Europeans to make their own rich, frothing Turkish coffee as it should be made. Worse still, they use the abominable French Bourbon and Martinique coffees instead of their pure, delicious native Mocha. Sometimes we used to amuse ourselves by "standing treat" to the bystanders. (I wonder how many cups of coffee an Arab *can* swallow in the twenty-four hours!) "*Ia kahouaji, zidna arbaia fenajel kahoua*" ("O seller of coffee, augment unto us four"—or whatever the number may be—"cups of coffee"). This would be acknowledged by a grave "*Issélmek men diaftek*" ("I thank thee for thy hospitality") from the recipients. Coffee is a cheap luxury—ten centimes a cup. The men are mostly smoking their long haschish pipes, and observe that if a man asks for a light, he does not say "*el nar*" ("fire," which would literally express his meaning), but "*el ájia*" ("peace"), because "*el nar*" being also used to express the fires of a certain region, where Sheitan and his angels will receive the wicked, it is not considered "good form" to allude to it in polite society. Neither must the flame be blown out with the breath, but extinguished by fanning with the hand; and finally, on taking leave of the company, one should say, "*Agáadou bes-slaáma*" ("Remain with peace"), to which they respond, "Peace go with you."

As for the houses which you pass, it is not easy to gain entrance, though occasionally you come across one—perhaps vacated long since by its impoverished Moorish owners—in which some European workman has set up shop. We strayed into one, I remember, where two Frenchmen sat making corks (the *chêne de liège* grows plentifully

in the woods here), and they were much amused at
our raptures over its spacious court and lofty pillars.
Another glorious old palace we found transformed
into a girls' school. But to a Moslem the house is
only less sacred than the mosque, and the door is
usually kept fast shut against inquisitive foreign
eyes. Once, however, a dear old woman, looking
down out of a *mousherarbiyah* about an inch
square, and seeing us casting longing looks at the
hermetically sealed doors, invited us to enter her
domain, a pretty little house, evidently very old.
It was naughty of her to admit the male part of the
contingent, and I blush to record that she was not
even veiled; but I don't think her morals suffered
to any considerable extent, for she was very nearly
as ancient as her house. Nor was she in danger of
being found out, for her husband, an *interprète
judiciaire*, was attending the assizes at Constantine,
and during his absence she amused herself by going
out and visiting her friends *ad lib.* She "liked to
run about and chatter," she said, "*comme les petites
poules,*" and to us it seemed a harmless taste;
though in reality, for a respectable Moorish matron,
it was, I fear, a shocking violation of *les conve-
nances.* She implored us to return another day and
have coffee, which we promised to do "if it pleased
God" (for note that it is considered to the last

A STREET IN THE ARAB QUARTER.

degree impious ever to speak in the future tense without adding the *incha Allah*"), but, needless to say, in that hopelessly puzzling rabbit warren, we were never able to light upon our dear old lady's house again.

But time passes, though I, for one, could linger in a Moorish town for ever, and often marvelled at hearing English people exclaim, " Oh, we only went into the Arab town once, and it was *so* dirty ; and we were driven away at once by the horrid smells." I feel disposed to inquire of such persons why they travel so far as Africa, when the contemplation of Belgrave Square, which is no doubt a very satisfying thing, would suit their tastes so much better. Smells ? Of course there are smells, my dear Sir or Madam ; what else did you expect ? But there are also strange sights, beautiful buildings, picturesque bits of colour, wonderful groups. If one could only transfer them instantaneously to canvas what an endless joy they would be to any one endowed with the artistic temperament !

I suppose there must always be the two types in this world, like the children in the old story of " Eyes and no Eyes," one noting only the commonplace and disagreeable, the other the beautiful and interesting objects in their path. But to *you*, dear reader, who *can* appreciate (or you would not have done me the honour to follow me through so many pages of these meanderings) all the wonders that we have come out to see,—to you I will whisper one word of counsel. Put some scent on your handkerchief before starting; I prefer Piver's "Essence Mystérieuse," which has a *soupçon* of Oriental attar of rose in its delicate composition, for to my mind perfumes should always blend harmoniously with their surroundings (imagine "Jockey Club" in the bath of Scheherezade!). Hold the said handkerchief to your nose, walk carefully, and thank God humbly that He has given you a spark of the poet-nature, which will enable you to seize, to enjoy to the utmost, and to grave upon your memory, the beauty that exists in the world which He has made. For that poet-nature is denied to many, who consequently, looking down, note only the filth and mire at their feet, instead of looking up and seeing the stars. I think they must lose much happiness out of their lives, don't you?

We traverse after this the Jewish quarter, the houses in which are principally modern and built in the French style. The synagogue is worth a visit on Saturdays, but otherwise there is nothing externally striking in the Israelitish camp. It is curious how the old antagonism between the children of the bondwoman and the children of the freewoman lingers even in these days. "If the French authorities would but give us leave," said an Arab to me once, "we would ask only three-quarters of an hour to clear every *ihoudi* (Jew) out of the town!"

Certainly the type of Hagar's son seems the nobler one. The men, with hardly any exceptions, are tall, stern, grand-looking, with their piercing eyes and their finely cut features. As they walk with splendid carriage and heads held erect, they seem to bear with them the everlasting memory of the wrongs of their father Ishmael as he lay panting in the desert, the unalterable destiny that has overtaken the seed of the "wild man" whose hand shall be against every man's until the end of time. The Jews and Jewesses, on the contrary, look respectively, the men crafty and greedy of gain, and the women, with their skinny faces and red-lidded eyes, poor put-upon creatures, with whom it is hard to connect the idea of the grand women of Holy Writ from Deborah and Judith, down to Our Lady, that fairest flower of womanhood.

Below this region lies the market and Place de Chartres, where we were photographed *en Arabe* (*vide* frontispiece) by M. Geiser, who makes a specialty of this. My costume, with its brocades and jewels, was lovely; but the shoes pinched, being clumsily made and of very coarse leather; and I envied my husband the nice red morocco, gold-embroidered top-boots which form part of the men's array. The Rue Bruce, in which the cathedral stands, is chiefly peopled by brass-workers, who make the pendant lamps which are such a decorative addition to mosques and houses here. Here also Madame Ben Aben has gathered round her some Moorish embroideresses, who turn out fairy fabrics covered with delicate stitches worked by their henna-tinted fingers; an art which once formed the chief occupation in the harems, but which is now principally kept alive owing to her efforts. Here is also the Archevêché, formerly the palace of the sultan's daughter (Dar bent-el-Sultan), and close by is the Musée-Bibliothèque, once part of the celebrated Djenina, or Palace of Gardens. Both these buildings are pretty nearly intact, and either will serve to give a general idea of a Moorish dwelling, which, though it may vary in magnificence, seldom varies in plan or style of architecture. The Archevêché has been restored in parts, and the principal apartments fitted up as reception-rooms, chapel, etc., for the Archbishop of Algeria. Perhaps, therefore, beautiful as it is with its ceilings and marble columns carved by Italian slaves, we had better cross over to the Museum, which has the merit of being absolutely untouched, and where there is a collection of fragments from other buildings now demolished. The plan, then, of these, as of all other Moorish and Turkish houses, is this. You first enter an outer court, with rooms off it, forming the men's quarters and servants' offices. Beyond it is the inner or women's court, which usually boasts a fountain in the centre. Columns, terminating in Moorish arches of the familiar "horse-shoe" shape, uphold a gallery with fretwork balustrades. The rooms opening on the four sides of this gallery are generally oblong in shape, with cupola-roofed bays receding from the further wall. In these recesses, which are raised a step above the rest of the room, stands a long, low, cushioned divan. Cupboards in the wall have the usual horse-shoe arch for outline, and are often possessed of panelled doors decorated in red and gold. Everywhere you walk upon the most exquisite tiles, of such delicately blended colour and design that they rival in effect the finest Persian carpets. The walls are also covered with these tiles up to a certain height, above which is the graceful frieze of pierced stucco-work, and over all the panelled ceiling of wood gilded and ornamented in conventional designs of subdued but rich colours. The windows giving on the outer world are, as we have seen, very tiny and high up, carefully barred, and more for air than to permit of being seen through. Often they are mere spaces in the masonry, filled with scraps of coloured glass, across which the pierced stucco spreads its lacy film. Light is principally derived from the court, and exercise is taken by the women on the flat roof, or "terrace," which is reached by a narrow staircase placed in one corner. This is the general plan of all such habitations, the large palaces having two or more courts, and perhaps three or sometimes even four stories, and ordinary dwellings one court, two stories, and of course less elaborate decoration. There are some fine Arabic and Persian manuscripts in the Museum.

Once more we emerge on the Boulevards, where old Salem, one of the celebrities of Algiers, is dancing and singing his crazy song of three notes to his queer Soudanese fiddle. If you bestow a ten-centime piece on him, he will insert it in his black nostril to amuse the bystanders; but though he scrapes his fiddle in all weathers for sous, he is, if report speaks truly, very rich, and owner of three houses.

And now, standing here, there stretches below us what is at once, perhaps, the brightest and yet the saddest part of Algiers—the harbour, with its surrounding buildings. Though modernized and macadamized now to the last degree, every inch we tread on has been trodden before us by countless poor suffering mortals, many of them our own fellow-countrymen. Who, think you, carved those exquisite renaissance wreaths of pendant fruits which smile at us from many a door lintel, in curious contrast to the Arabian architecture round them? Christian slaves. Who, when Khair-ed-din succeeded in ousting the Spaniards from the Peñon, built on it that shapely lighthouse tower, with its white walls outlined by bands of bright tiles? Christian slaves again. Who constructed the jetty that connects it with the mainland? Twenty thousand Christian slaves. Who lived in that beautiful old house—now the Amirauté—with its Moorish fountain and Arabic inscriptions carved on white marble? Cruel Turkish taskmasters, who looked well to it that the lashes were not spared.

Yes, over that water, crowded now with fishing-smacks, passenger-steamers, and luxurious yachts, the corsairs came with captured prize ships, whose plunder should enrich the dey's palace; while Antonio stood watching vainly at home for the fleet that held his ventures, and the stout sailors who would never cheer at sight of land again. Think of the gentle maids hauled roughly up there to the pasha's harem; of the haughty knights with their backs bending beneath base burdens; of the fainting oarsmen chained to the galleys in that scorching sun, their flesh eaten into by the gyves. Think of it, you who sail the seas in safety now! Sometimes those in Europe found means to buy them back. There is an old print called "Le Rachat de l'Esclave" which depicts a great lady with her pages round her, standing on the seashore to welcome back her poor lord, who has just landed from the ransoming ship, while his faithful dog springs forward to greet him. I have in my possession a curious sermon, preached in London in 1637, by one Fitz-Geffrey, "On the Duty of showing Mercy towards Prisoners, especially to our Unhappy Countrymen now Captives in Barbarie." Indeed, in England collections for their ransom were frequently made in the churches at this time; but it could have been only a drop in the ocean, and for one that was rescued, how many were left behind?* And what the tortures they must have suffered—tortures so terrible that to avoid them they would even abjure the faith of their fathers—who can tell? There is an old service in the Anglican liturgy which bears significantly on this part of the question.

I believe it is not now generally known that

* In the Roman Church, also, noble work was done by the Fathers of the Redemptionist Order, founded by Jean de Matha expressly for the succour of captives of that faith.

among the occasional offices of the Church of England there exists one set forth by authority in the year 1635, and entitled, " A Form of Penance or Reconciliation for a Renegado or Apostate from the Christian Church to Turcism." * The need for it arose briefly thus. Most of the English slaves set free by means of the money thus charitably collected returned at once to their native shores, and Matthew Wren, Bishop of Ely in the reign of Charles I., in whose diocese a large number of them settled, found, on inquiring into their spiritual welfare, that many had been reduced under extremity of torture to apostatize from the faith. He hastened to inform Laud, Archbishop of Canterbury, and the king of this fact; with the result that the archbishop, aided by himself, the Bishop of Winchester, and other prelates, drew up the service in question. Being of interest both as a liturgical curiosity and in connection with the present subject, I venture to give a few extracts from it.

The first rubrics ordain that—

" *The offender's Conviction be first judicially heard before the Bishop of the Diocese, that . . . thereupon an Excommunication be decreed and denounced both in the Cathedral and Parish Church . . . and the Form of his Penance enjoined him.*"

---

* The complete office may be found in "Hierurgia Anglicana," in Wilkins's "Concilia" (1737), and in Jeremy Collier's "Ecclesiastical History," etc.

And that his parish priest

"*Have frequent Conference with the Party in private, lay open and aggravate the heinousness of this Sin . . . and see whether his Conscience be troubled with any other grievous Crime, that so he may be the better fitted for Absolution of all together.*

"*. . . The next Sunday following let the Offender be appointed to stand all the time of Divine Service and Sermon in the Porch, [order must be taken that Boys and idle People flock not about him] of the Church . . . in a penitent fashion in a white Sheet with a white Wand in his Hand, his Head uncovered, his Countenance dejected. . . . And when the People come in and go out of the Church, let him . . . humbly crave their Prayers . . . in this Form.*

"*Good Christians, remember in your Prayers a poor wretched Apostate or Renegado.*

"*The second Sunday let him stand in the Church Porch in his penitential Habit as before, and then after the* Te Deum *ended, let him be brought in by one of the Church-Wardens so far as the west side of the Font . . . there let him . . . kneel . . . and make his Submission . . . in the Form following.*

"*O Lord God of Heaven and Earth, be merciful to me a most wretched Sinner. [This said, let him smite his breast three times.] I confess, O Lord, I have justly deserved to be utterly renounced by Thee, because I have yielded to renounce my Saviour. O God, forgive me this heinous and horrible Sin . . . and let me, upon Thy gracious Pardon . . . be restored to the Rights and Benefit of this Blessed Sacrament which I have so wickedly abjured, and be received, though most unworthy, into Thy gracious Favour and the Communion of Thy faithful People, even for Thy great Mercy Sake, in Jesus Christ my blessed Lord and Saviour.*

"*Which done, let him in an humble and devout Manner kiss the bottom Stone of the Font, strike his Breast, and presently depart into the Church Porch as before. The third Sunday, let him at the beginning of Divine Service be brought into the Body of the Church . . . where the Minister . . . shall ask the Penitent publickly, whether he have found a true and earnest Remorse in his Soul for this Sin.*"

Here follows a set form whereby the penitent makes public confession in the presence of the congregation; after which the priest enjoins them to consider " the weakness of our frail Nature, when it is over-pressed with violence and extremity of Torments; and both to commiserate his fearful Apostacy, and to encourage and comfort him in this happy return to Christ and His Church."

"*Here let the Penitent kneel down again Eastward . . . and say this:—*
"O my Soul, bless the Lord:
"Blessed be the Father of Mercies, and the God of all Consolation:
"Blessed be the Lord Jesus, the Son of God, the Saviour of the World:
"Blessed be the Holy Spirit, God the Holy Ghost:
"Blessed be the Holy Trinity, one God everlasting:
"Blessed be the Holy Catholic Church, and all you the Servants of the Lord Jesus Christ.
"The Name of God be blessed evermore for the Assembly of His Saints and for the Divine Ordinances of His most holy Word and Sacraments; and of His heavenly Power committed to His holy Priest in His Church for the Reconciliation of Sinners unto Himself and the absolving them from all their Iniquity. Lo! here I upon the bended Knees of my Body and Soul, most humbly beg the Assistance of all your Christian Prayers and the Benefit of that His holy Ordinance. And I humbly beseech you, Sir, as my ghostly Father, a Priest of God, to receive me into . . . the Bosom of the Church by loosing me from the bonds of my grievous Sins.

"*Then let the Priest come forth to him and . . . say as is prescribed in the Book of Common Prayer, thus:*
"Our Lord Jesus Christ, Who has left Power to His Church to absolve all Sinners which truly repent and believe in Him, of His great mercy forgive thee thine Offences: and by His Authority committed to me, I absolve thee from this heinous Crime of Renunciation and from all other thy Sins, in the Name of the Father, and of the Son, and of the Holy Ghost. Amen."

After this the rubric directs that "the Priest turning Eastward kneel down in the same Place, the Penitent kneeling behind him," after which the priest is to "take him up, and take away his white Sheet and Wand." And after an exhortation, the concluding rubric states that the penitent is then "openly promised" that he "be admitted to the Holy Sacrament, for which let him be directed to prepare himself. And when he receives, let him make a solemn Oblation, according to his Ability, after the Order set down in the Service Book." *

I wonder when this service was last used? Probably seldom later than 1655, after which date — thanks to Blake—the Algerines were taught to leave British ships alone. But how vividly it makes one realize it all. Imagine such a state of things as enforced apostacy arising nowadays for English subjects, and the Archbishop of Canterbury of 189— having to set forth special offices to meet the wants of returning penitents to the sheepfold! And let us be thankful that we live in times when the power of Islam is at least scotched, though not yet killed. It began to wane considerably in North Africa by the end of the seventeenth century. First

---

* Those English subjects who kept the faith were at one time ministered to by a noble Anglican priest, the Rev. Devereux Spratt, who—as Mr. Lane-Poole relates—"was captured off Youghal as he was crossing only from Cork to Bristol, and so distressed was the good man at the miserable condition of many of the slaves at Algiers, that when he was ransomed he yielded to their entreaties, and stayed a year or two longer to comfort them with his holy offices. . . . In the sad circle of the captives marriages and baptisms took place, and some are recorded in the parish register of Castnell, Lancashire, as having been performed in 'Argeir' by Mr. Spratt."—"The Barbary Corsairs," p. 266).

the French, then the Dutch, and successively other nations, either by victorious combat or monetary payments, succeeded in getting their flags respected by the Algerines; but the Spaniards and the Italian States, till as late as 1816, still suffered cruelly from the power of the savage pirates of Barbary.

CHAPTER III.

ARABS "CHEZ EUX."

Arabs *chez eux*—Their families and *fêtes*—Sidi Mustafa and his home—My first introduction to kouss-kouss—A Moorish wedding feast—An Arab conjurer—The scorpion-eating Aïssonas—The Ouled-Naïls—The Lahabin-Bessiouf—The Negro dancers—Mahommed ben Hussein Cherif—Zorah—I study Arabian music under her auspices—An evening at the Marabout's—Mahommed ben Ahmed—Little Fatma.

My best friend was Sidi Mustafa; and a more perfect gentleman it would be hard to find. He was introduced to us by a French friend of ours, and promised to take us to see an Arab wedding feast, if we would meet him at a certain *kahoua* at five o'clock.

Tall, stately, with an aquiline nose, finely chiselled aristocratic features, and a short iron-grey beard trimmed in a point; his high snow-white head-dress wound round with many a mingled strand of camel's-hair wool; on one shapely hand an antique silver ring, and his burnous hanging in graceful folds, Sidi Mustafa stalked slowly along with the peculiarly dignified sailing motion which belongs to his people alone, and which they seem to share with the camels of their native desert. We stumbled along meekly in his wake, conscious of not presenting an equally good appearance; for to mount a steep labyrinth of very narrow streets, paved with rough cobbles, and broken by steps at irregular distances; jostled by strings of pack-laden donkeys; slipping on refuse, and in danger of upsetting on one hand a sweetmeat-seller and his stall, and on the other a shoemaker sitting cross-legged at his work, is not an easy matter for the unaccustomed European. I pulled his burnous once, and gasped out, "*Ed-dar baïda, sidi?*" ("Is the house far off?"); but he reassured us on that point, and stalked on once more with his splendid head in the air, looking more like a camel than ever. Once he met a friend nearly as handsome as himself, and, without a word on either side, these two tall, bearded Arabs fell on each other's neck and kissed each other silently, and then passed on their several ways.

At last we reached a portal with the hand of Fatma* carved on it to avert the evil eye. Here he halted, and invited us to follow him into a cool court with lovely tiles. We beheld a curtain being

---

* The Prophet's daughter. It is usual to call girl-babies after her, with the (optional) addition of another name.

suddenly unlooped on the opposite side of the court, and heard a swift scuttling as of frightened hens. It was merely the ladies of the establishment hiding themselves, and, of course, we took no notice of it; for it is considered the height of rudeness to ask questions or betray curiosity about your host's domestic relations. "Is thy household well?" is the nearest approach permissible to asking after the health of his womankind. By-and-by, however, he graciously condescended to fetch his wife, who came with her youngest olive branch in her arms. This was a special favour, which, of course, could be accorded to Europeans alone, and then only by a few enlightened Arabs, who have arrived at the conclusion that such innocent sociability is within the range of things possible. Perhaps our host had less hesitation, as his wife was exceedingly plain, and not in her first youth; but had an Arab arrived on the scene, she would have fled immediately. The baby, Hourīya, was a beautiful child, whose long black eyelashes swept her cheek while she smiled pensively. If she grows up as lovely as she promised to do, she will indeed merit her name, which signifies "Little Fairy."

Kouss-kouss was then brought in in a large bowl, which was placed on a low stand, round which we all sat in a circle. There are no plates; but every one feeds out of the dish. The correct way is to eat with one's fingers, but we were allowed wooden spoons in deference to our prejudices. The kousskouss on this occasion was sweet, and one tired of it after a few mouthfuls; but the *relevé* kind, consisting of meat and chicken shredded up, very highly seasoned, and mixed with the fine semolina which in all cases forms the groundwork of kousskouss, is a most delicious dish. Between every spoonful we were pressed to drink the sour milk placed beside every one. This is considered a great delicacy, and we had to put our lips to it with as little anguish as possible in our countenances; for one must always avoid refusing anything that is offered. Coffee followed, and then the Sid proceeded to show us all his Arabic books. Of these he had a great number, many of them in manuscript, and containing all sorts of curious puzzles made by writing the letters of a name in different ways. Madame Mustafa then produced a kind of spinning-wheel used in preparing the silk of which the *haïcks* are made, and showed us her cupboard full of quince-jam, prepared in the native fashion. Finally, as time was passing, we ventured to inquire, "And the wedding, sidi?" Whereupon it transpired that the feast had been postponed for a week, when he would take us to it; but meanwhile, with the wonderful tact and courtesy of his race, he had not wished to dismiss us disappointedly from the rendezvous, and so had brought us to partake of his own hospitality instead. He returned the visit at our villa a few days afterwards, and often came to see us subsequently, when he would sit in the verandah and drink coffee with us; and when he found that I loved their Eastern tales, full of sultans and beautiful princesses, of slaves and jewels, he used to stay telling them to me by the hour, and patiently waiting while I wrote them down; and if we came to a word I did not understand, we helped ourselves out by the aid of the French-Arabic dictionary.

The following week the wedding feast alluded to above came off in good earnest, and very varied were the entertainments provided for the guests. We found ourselves on arriving, piloted by Mustafa, in the midst of a dense throng which filled the inner court of the house. In a central space stood the jugglers and other performers; the four sides of the square round them were packed with spectators, jammed together as tightly as sardines; and on a divan slightly elevated above the rest sat the host, whom every guest on entering or departing embraced silently.

When we arrived the floor was held by an Arab

conjurer, who was occupied in producing dates
apparently from nowhere and handing them round
to the company, keeping up an incessant trembling
movement of his whole body all the while. The
Aïssouas, or dervishes, followed, ascetic thin-faced
men, with facial expressions verging on madness, who
swallowed, or pretended to swallow, live scorpions.
As each scorpion disappeared down their throats
a shrill cry arose of " You-you-you-you-you-ee,"
as sharp and highly pitched as the scream of a
railway whistle when the train enters a tunnel.
This proceeded from the gallery over our heads
whence the women were watching the revels. They
are always allowed on such occasions to lean over
the balustrade and survey the scene, and their
invariable note of applause is an essential part of
the proceedings. But woe be to one of those
bearded Arabs sitting impassively below who should
dare to transgress the code of honour by raising
so much as an eyelid in their direction. A Frenchman told me that once an Arab host, seeing him
incautiously glancing upwards, said severely, " You
may open your eyes to look upon the ground and
around you, but you must not look above;" and
not one of the native guests would dream of betray-
ing the slightest interest, though the gallery above
is as full of movement and *chuchotements* as the trees

overhead are with the noise of birds in nesting time. All through the various performances a row of cross-legged musicians kept up a never-ending rhythmic accompaniment on flutes, derbonkas, tom-toms, and guitars. When tired, a fresh relay relieved the others. The derbonkas are large vase-shaped gourds, hollowed out and covered at one end with parchment; and they supply the regular "thum-thum" of the bass notes, much as the 'cello does with us. The flutes emit shrill treble sounds. The tambourines have to be kept constantly heated over a charcoal brazier which burns on the floor, and serves also for the smokers to light their pipes by. To this music the dervishes danced, flinging themselves madly about and shaking all over. With the aid of a huge negro, who stood by acting as master of the ceremonies, they gradually, without stopping their dance, divested themselves of their underclothing, retaining only the outer garment, a thin white linen cloak; and at last, streaming with perspiration and excited almost to frenzy, they fell heavily on the floor, where they lay motionless. I anxiously inquired of Sidi Mustafa if they were ill, but was met by a reassuring "No, no." Finally they cooled down and picked themselves up, to be succeeded by the Ouled-Naïls * with their accustomed

* See Appendix A.

danse du ventre, and afterwards by the "Lahabin-Bessiouf," or *danseurs du sabre*, from the desert, who made graceful play with their swords, pretending to pierce each other, yet ever eluding the thrusts. Then, to quicker music, came forward a number of negroes, who, joining hands, romped madly in a circle, rather like an exaggerated edition of the Kitchen Lancers. The negroes in Algeria are chiefly the descendants of those formerly imported by the Turks from M'zab and the Soudan to act as slaves; they now mix on equal terms with the Arabs, and are always gay and friendly. Many adhere to their own ancient religion, and curious visitors who do not mind horrors can go to see their "Sacrifice of the Hen," which takes place frequently on the seashore. I never went, not caring to see an unfortunate live fowl cut into small pieces, to be thrown into the sea, whilst auguries are drawn from the way in which its blood falls to the ground.

These performances having occupied some hours, we had not time to wait for kouss-kouss to be served; so after I had been admitted to a brief interview upstairs with the *aroussa* (bride), a graceful timid girl of about thirteen, bowed down with bangles, we took leave of our host, who looked intensely bored by the whole show. No doubt there is a want of variety in Oriental amusements, though they would take some time to pall upon Europeans who come fresh to such bizarre and unaccustomed sights.

We did not see the bridegroom, who would not come to fetch his bride till night, but who had been before the cadi at the beginning of the ceremonies. The young lady in question was decidedly pretty; but I think the conventional ideas as to the loveliness of Mauresques greatly exaggerated; for when visiting a number of unveiled women in their apartments, I have generally found a large preponderance of them really plain, with coarse skins, large mouths, and irregular features; and as an Arab is never allowed to see his wife unveiled till after the ceremonies are concluded, I fancy *ces pauvres messieurs* must sometimes feel a little disappointed!

Mahommed ben Hussein Cherif, whose acquaintance we made about this time, was an excessively handsome young Moor, with a long pale refined face and charming manners. The "Cherif"* after his name denotes that he is "the s*k*ion of a noble house," as I once heard a north-country farmer call the Parliamentary candidate at an electioneering meeting.

---

* Those elevated to the Turkish nobility conferred by the Imperial Porte are designated "Aouzir." "Cherif" denotes the Arab nobility, the special right of those who can prove their descent from the family of the Prophet, and who consequently wear a green turban.

COURT OF A HOUSE IN OLD ALGIERS.

He had a vast store of anecdotic and traditional lore, and to him I am chiefly indebted for the legends of the Algerian Marabouts, which will be found in the next chapter.

Finding also that I was interested in the curious music of his people, he arranged for me an interview with a clever professional *chanteuse*, by name Zorah, who sang and played brilliantly on a highly decorated native guitar. She afterwards accompanied herself on the piano, to help me in gaining a better idea of the compositions. Every song has a long prelude, and an equally long interlude is introduced between each verse. As the songs usually contain at least thirty verses, it will be seen that to hear even one to the end occupies some two hours or more; but that is of no importance to the Arabs. They never hurry, and indeed everything in their languid lives seems done with a view to killing time.

There is little light and shade, and no absolute tune (at least to our ears), but the harmonies are well arranged, and the orchestration profoundly clever. The instruments being cruder than ours, their varying characteristics strike more strongly on the ear. There is a great deal of "contrary motion;" the unprepared seventh seems to be the discord most frequently used, and "passing-notes," turns, and *appoggiaturas* embellish the upper parts incessantly. The bass often remains unchanged throughout an entire phrase, while the treble is performing most unaccountable gymnastics. I should say that rhythm forms the principal element in their music, replacing that of melody in ours; and from careful study of the performances of Zorah and others, I gathered that the song and its accompaniment are two perfectly distinct things. In the latter, the treble usually ranges at about two octaves above middle C, the bass an octave below it; and midway between these starts the singer, on notes apparently quite independent of the rest, and with a separate set of rambling twists and turns, which reduce the listener to a state of hopeless bewilderment. The voice production is faulty according to our ideas, having a shrill and "throaty" effect.

Considering that there is no perceptible air to serve as a guide, nothing to mark time but the regular beat of the bass, no written copies to learn from (musical notation being apparently unknown to this nation, whose music has been handed down orally for hundreds of years), the unflagging aplomb of their performances is little short of phenomenal. In their concerted pieces there is no conductor, the musicians sitting cross-legged in a row or semicircle; yet from start to finish the time is kept as though by a metronome. No one forgets, no one breaks down, there is never a false note; the flutes scream shrilly, the fiddles scrape, the gourds and tom-toms beat out deep muffled strokes, and the concert is as ably gone through as though under the direction of a Richter or a Randegger.

I have often wondered that no great musician has ever analyzed and transcribed this Arab music. Perhaps some day a student will arise—the Max Müller of harmony—who will formulate and bring within our reach the varying musical tongues of strange nations. For has not every people, however outlandish, its own special language of song, which is surely as worthy of being interpreted as the spoken words which men group together in grammars and garner up in dictionaries? And if ever that day comes I venture to assert that amongst the most interesting of all will be the music of the Moors; not only for its inherent beauty, but also for the all-pervading, never-dying influence it has had on the glorious, wild, intoxicating music of Spain.

Their songs are mostly worded at great length in praise of some beautiful "light of the harem," separate stanzas being devoted to the enumeration of her charms; *i.e.* the glories of her eyes, cheeks, lips, etc. Others are ballads commemorating some historical event, and to show the antiquity of these I append a verse, roughly Englished, from one which Zorah sang, in which the narrator tells the tale of the taking of Granada to a listener whom he addresses as " Saphir."

> "Ia (O) Saphir! we were in a castle,
>   In a town where all was good;
> We were dancing and singing,
> But Spain has desired to conquer us;
>   And it must needs be that we
>   Have become incapable of fighting,
> For our country, our Granada is taken from us."

There is something piteous in the wailing songs which rise unaltered from the lips of these singers still, as though Time had turned his hourglass back to the days of Ferdinand the Catholic, when such plaints must have sounded freshly in the ranks of the reconquered conquerors.

At length, after spoiling several sheets of music-paper in my unskilled attempts to write down the baffling sounds, Zorah swathed her guitar in many wrappings of musk-scented stuffs, and her own head in the customary *haïck*, or face-veil; for these musicians, though necessarily regarded by the Arabs as *déclassées* from the contact with the public into which their profession brings them, go abroad as carefully shrouded as the most respectable of their sex. I laughingly asked her how I should ever know her again if I met her in the street, as all

Mauresques look more or less alike when veiled. "Mais Madame me reconnaîtra facilement, parce que je suis louche," said poor Zorah; and in effect she squinted horribly. I have seen many Moorish women with this defect, which is probably the result of a want of careful surveillance in childhood.

My friend Mahommed ben Hussein very kindly procured us an invitation to a rich feast, given in honour of a great Marabout; and on this occasion I spent a most agreeable evening in the women's apartments. Perhaps a description of it may be found not uninteresting, especially as to travellers of the sterner sex such experiences are, of course, denied.*

At about nine p.m. Sidi Mahommed came to fetch us; and after driving as far as the roads permitted, we were forced to leave the carriage and proceed on foot up winding ways to the door of hospitality. In trying to enter an Arab house it is always a

---

* At Algiers, however, "la belle Fatma," who lives in the Rue de la Révolution, receives European visitors of both sexes. She is, needless to remark, a *demi-mondaine*; but notwithstanding this fact it is considered quite permissible to visit her, and droves of tourists are "personally conducted" to view her house and jewels, and drink coffee with her at so much per head! She will organize native dances at her house, under the auspices of Messrs. Cook and Son; and perhaps to ladies whose stay is too short to admit of their becoming acquainted with the better class of native families, or to men—who are of course completely debarred from ever doing so—it may be useful in conveying a faint idea of a Moorish interior. For my part, however, I failed to find in her dwelling what one guide-book describes as "the thorough illusion of the East."

matter of uncertainty as to whether one will succeed in gaining admittance or not. First, a series of loud knocks on the outer door (innocent of bells) must be given. Sometimes no notice whatever is taken, and the knocker is forced to go disconsolately away. Should the inmates be inclined to receive, an old woman-servant's voice will be heard questioning from some hidden region. If reassured by the answer, the bolts will be withdrawn—sometimes not till after prolonged parleying; but an interval must be allowed for the opener to retire discreetly from the gaze of profane men.

When at last we did find ourselves on the right side of the portal, and had been duly presented to the gentlemen of the party, my husband and Mahommed ben Hussein were taken by them to the rooms of the inner court, while I was directed to the foot of a staircase where a very handsome Mauresque was waiting to conduct me up to the precincts of womankind.

Looking back on it now, my memory conjures up a long low room, sumptuously carpeted and cushioned. Priceless Moorish tables and *étagères* met the eye everywhere, some painted, some inlaid, and all really antique—a boon in these days when so much modern stuff drugs the market. The room was lighted by the pendant brass lamps familiar to frequenters of "Oriental" warehouses, and by monster candles of purest wax, twisted, painted, and decorated like the Paschal candle in a church. Some of these were fixed in sconces, some standing upright on the floor. The ancient rugs were of the most exquisite designs and colours, and "all the perfumes of Araby" filled the air. Lying in attitudes of languid grace on divans round the room, were about twenty women, some young and lovely, some old and wrinkled; but the clothes of all of them were a dream. Such brocades, such clinking of anklets and frontlets, such glistening of jewels! The hostess herself—if so she might be called, for this was the Marabout's house, not her own—was a young woman of wonderful beauty. She was giving the feast in accordance with a vow made to the said Marabout, to whose prayers she owed the fulfilment of her wish for another child,* and this day the infant had been taken for the first time to the bath, a great occasion in the lives of Arab babies. Having been duly led up to her and presented by my conductress (for an Eastern hostess does not rise or come forward to receive you), the young mother exhibited the

* When the Mahommedans wish to obtain any favour from Allah, they ask the all-powerful prayers of a Marabout, to whom they vow gifts should the prayer be granted. The poor give candles and other trifles, but with the rich it is customary to promise a feast, which is then usually held actually in the house of the Marabout, so that any money collected from the guests may be placed at his disposal for the poor.

heroine of the occasion to me with great pride. Although only six weeks old, the young lady had beautifully formed features and the true Eastern almond eyes, which were fringed with long lashes, and seemed already full of languishing softness. The blackness of her baby brows was already deepened by dyes, her tiny shells of finger-nails reddened with henna. Her little skull was bound tightly with rich silks and gauzes, and the remaining inches of her small person were enveloped in a mass of glittering stuffs, and covered with jewels. I was lost in admiration of her and her dear little four-year-old brother Mahommed. This tiny namesake of the Prophet strutted about with the air of a small pasha. He wore a miniature kaftan and vest of flowered brocade on a mauve ground. Little clustered curls adorned his crown, which was uncovered—I know not why; but he is the only Arab, large or small, whom I have ever seen bare-headed. He was too small to be jealous of the baby sister who was the cause of such great rejoicings, and seemed to be making the most of the notice bestowed on him by the ladies, from whose gallery a few more years will see him excluded.

Coffee and sweetmeats were brought in and placed on a low mother-of-pearl table. There were delicious little *pralinés* cakes, biscuits flavoured with ratafia, and bonbons which melted in the mouth. Yielding to hospitable entreaties, I "sampled" a number, and found them each more delicious than the other. After this some of the ladies conversed with me in a mixture of French and Arabic. They brought out their work for my inspection—delicate embroideries, and less lovely arrangements in white thread, distantly related to our old-fashioned "tatting." My diamond rings interested them much; for, though they possess fine stones, the natives do not set them clear, and they lose half their brilliant effect by being so deeply embedded in the gold. A row of seated female *alatia* (musicians) lined one wall of the apartment, talking in laughing asides to each other, and now heating their tambourines over the charcoal braziers placed for that purpose, now breaking out into songs for the amusement of the company. All this time there was a continual *va et vient* of guests, some taking leave with silent salutes, others shuffling off their shoes in the doorway as they arrived on the scene. I felt rather shy under the scrutiny of so many dark eyes; but, for the most part, the new-comers, after their first curiosity was satisfied, took no further notice of me, and I sat surveying them apart, like a shade from the other world—

"Revisiting the glimpses of the moon."

They chattered amongst themselves; they wove chains of orange-blossom buds (one which was given to me I have now, all dried and brown, but scented still); they smoked; they nibbled sweetmeats; and, lastly, they danced, for the ladies are frequently taught to dance as gracefully as the Almées, though, of course, in their case the spectators are confined to their own sex.* One splendid creature, with finely cut features, flashing eyes, gorgeous trousers of antique red-and-gold brocade, and beautiful rings, gave me especial pleasure. Heavens, how she danced! Now she swam; now she rose; now, advancing step by step, she waved her head from side to side, her white arms upholding a gauzy scarf the while. Anon, her head and still uplifted arms alike held motionless, her eyes bent down, she seemed to watch with pleasure the *déhanchement* of her nether limbs, which quivered into waves of graceful movement. And ever the shrill cries of "You-you-you-you-you-you-you-ee" rose higher, and the young mother who gave the feast threw her in jest a golden coin such as they fling in earnest to the dancing girls. Never stop-

* "La danse n'est point le privilège exclusif des femmes galantes. Toutes les femmes connaissent plus ou moins l'art de se déhancher en agitant des mouchoirs au-dessus de leur tête."—Lieut.-Col. Villot, ancien chef de Bureau Arabe, "Mœurs et Coutumes de l'Algérie," p. 172.

ing for an instant, she caught it, and poised it on her uplifted forehead, and still danced on, never altering the angle of her stag-like head, nor letting the gold piece fall. These voluptuous movements must have lasted a full quarter of an hour, when at last she sank breathless on the divan, while the others flung chains of orange-blossom round her neck, and plied her with coffee.

I could have stayed for ever feasting my senses there; but, alas! the time came when I felt I must tear myself away from this strange chamber of dreams. So, bidding farewell to the assembled ladies with the regulation kisses and oft-repeated "Bes-slámas," I delivered myself up to my former conductress, who piloted me along the moonlit galleries, down narrow spiral staircases, and across the tiled court, finally leaving me at the door of the room where the men were entertaining my husband; and, behold! I was in the waking world once more.

Do you remember the old mysterious romances of the date of "The Castle of Otranto," in which the hero is suddenly visited by unknown masks, who blindfold and conduct him silently along tortuous ways—which, try as he will, he can never in after life retrace—to some gloomy palace? Through postern gates, up secret stairs, he is brought to a room hung with arras, where the bandage is lifted from his eyes. Having therein borne his part in whatever strange adventure—be it the aid of a distracted beauty, the slaughter of a miscreant knight, the witnessing of a document of untold value, or what not—forms the basis of the tale, he is once more blindfolded and led away. His speechless guides place him in the coach which awaits them, and he is borne to his home, bound by strange oaths never to divulge what he has seen that night; and, finally, left alone to ponder and puzzle over the unfathomable occurrences which will haunt him for the rest of his life.

Very much like this did I feel when my "lady guide" made off, leaving me "planted there," as the French say. I pinched my arm, to see if I was really awake, for my head felt in a whirl; gathered up my garland of orange-buds, and, hearing familiar voices within, summoned up courage to knock and enter.

The Marabout had not returned from Biskra. This fact would not have been surprising in the case of any one *but* a Marabout, as there were no trains due at that time of night! But then, you see, Marabouts do not depend on such inconsiderable trifles as trains; for they can travel miraculously through space, and we were gravely told that he might arrive from the desert at any moment to grace the feast. The wheels of his chariot tarried too long for our patience, however; and, though the Arabs were prepared to keep up the affair till four a.m., we beat a retreat, descending through moonlit streets to where the carriage awaited us on the outskirts of civilization; and, long past midnight, I reached home to sleep and dream over again the strange experiences of that evening.

Amongst our friends in a humbler grade of life was Mahommed ben Ahmed, the boatman in whose felucca we were wont to go on water-excursions. The felucca, a clean little craft, was named *Le Pilot*, and many a pleasant sail did we have with her. Poor man! He told us that once upon a time he lived in a pretty house up near the Kasbah, and had a young wife whom he loved passionately. But she had died, and now, having bought this boat, he and his son had to lodge in a European house near the quay; and he had sent his young daughter to live with her grandmother, for it was not permitted that womenfolk should dwell under the same roof with "Roumis." He said, moreover, that now, when his work was done, he spent his time playing damma in the kahoua, often not going to bed till past midnight; "*for*," he added with pathetic significance, "*for me, the nights are long now.*"

Mahommed ben Ahmed was of an honest and ruddy countenance. He had donned the ordinary navy-blue serge coat of mariners, though retaining the Moslem fez and baggy white trousers. He told us that he had to pay forty francs yearly to renew his boat-license, and heavy taxes besides; and that though in the time of the Empire the Arabs were very happy under French rule, under the Republic times are bad for the poor.

A curious example of the complete distrustfulness of Mahommedan husbands in the fidelity of their spouses was elicited by my question as to whether his wife when living ever used to go out. Though he had evidently adored her, he replied, "*Never*, unless she went to the mosque, or to visit her relations, and then only on condition that my mother accompanied her. Under her own mother's escort I would not have trusted her"!

He was a strict Musulman, and though he sometimes accepted provisions from our luncheon-basket, was very particular never to touch ham or grease in any form, even with his fingers. But once I really think he was nearly becoming a convert to our creed. It happened on this wise. One Friday morning he presented himself at our villa with the announcement that the wind was favourable for a long-planned excursion to Cap Matifou. When we were safely on board, and not till then, did I remember that it was Friday; and I laughingly asked him if he shared the Christian seaman's objection to put forth to sea on that day. He said, "No; for with us it is a feast day, the day of prayer" (*el nar el djemâa*). I said, "With us, on the contrary, it is a sad day, and by many accounted an unlucky one; for on it Our Lord was killed by the Ihoud. [N.B.—All Moslems hate the Jews.] And thou shalt see, O Mahommed, that perhaps to-day we shall not prosper." I said this half in jest; but sure enough, ere we were well out on the blue bay across whose waters so many captives have been washed to the feet of the cruel deys, the wind dropped, and we rowed in a dead calm. There was nothing for it but to give up the enterprise; but it would have been too ignominious to return to land before the day was well begun. So we anchored for lunch, only to discover that the basket had been packed minus salt, butter, or sugar. Later on the anchor was found to have become embedded in a rock, to the despair of Mahommed; for to have bought another would have made a large hole in his savings. However, it was fortunately dislodged after a long struggle. After this, it occurred to us to while away the still early hours by fishing in the harbour; but not a morsel of bait could we obtain from the neighbouring boats. At last, getting rather "riled" at the persistent contrariness of fate, I insisted on being rowed to shore, and sent Mahommed up to the Pêcheries to buy bait, after which we essayed our luck, only to be baffled once more. For whereas on other occasions the boat had been quickly peopled by the delicious little fish of the bay (name unknown, but peace to their bones, for I have eaten many a good dishful of them!), on this day not one could we hook. Eventually we returned to shore, very much disgusted with our chapter of accidents; and as I landed, I said, "Ia Mahommed, thou seest that Friday is not a fortunate day for the Christians." He cordially assented, seeming duly impressed with the fact that the Christ must have been a very great Marabout,* and one thing is certain, namely, that he never suggested to us to go for a trip with him on a Friday again.

And whose is this little voice at my feet crying "Madame, donne un sou"? Ah, is it you, my little Fatma, my child-friend? and did you think I had forgotten you? She popped up in front of us at a mosque door one day, a little *gamine* clad in a ragged *haïck*, too young to be veiled, but not too young to know that she had glorious eyes and to

---

* As indeed all good Mahommedans believe. They speak of Him as "His Holiness Jesus, on whom be peace."

use them ruthlessly. That child was a picture. She saw that we had taken a fancy to her, the friendship was cemented by lumps of sugar from a neighbouring café, and from that moment, go where I would—on the highest ramparts of the Kasbah, on the lowest step of the quay—Fatma would sidle up with her picturesque little head on one side, her palm outstretched and her eyes doing immense execution, as she droned out the inevitable refrain, "Madame, donne un sou!" Sometimes I would say, "*Elioum ma andisch draham, ia Fatma. Rodoua incha Allah niatinek el sourdi*" ("To-day I have no money, O Fatma. To-morrow, if it shall please Allah, I will give thee a sou"); and on the morrow she would turn up as indefatigably as ever, in search of the promised coin.

One morning, on the Boulevard, I beheld a seated circle of children (literal "street Arabs"), and coming nearer, I found Mademoiselle Fatma in the midst of the admiring group, dancing—yes, actually dancing the *danse du ventre!* She had "got the hang of it" exactly; and the monkey was going solemnly through all the movements like the most hardened Ouled-Naïl of them all; while the children round her shrilled "You-you-you-ee," as the women do when they look on at feasts. I have watched the regular Biskri girls dance it, and even ladies, as we have seen, in the privacy of their own apartments, where no curious man might peep; but the most bizarre edition I ever saw was that rendered by little Fatma (she could not have been more than eight) as she danced it on the Boulevard with childish gravity—and let us hope innocence—in the full glare of the noonday sun. Ah, well! It were best to dance on, little Fatma, while you may; for in a few short years your mother will call you in and veil you, and thrust your little feet into those hard shoes, which hurt one's feet; and never more will you be permitted to gambol in the sunshine, or beg sous from the passers-by. For you will have come to the age when all girls, rich or poor, must be veiled; and ever after you will only go out on rare occasions to the cemetery or the mosque, sedately following some older woman. Perhaps if some man has money enough to satisfy your parents' greed, he will buy you, and make you his wife and slave, toy with you for a few short weeks, then neglect or ill-treat you; perhaps even divorce you and turn you out-of-doors, as is too often the way with Arab husbands. Who can tell what tears may fall from those bright eyes in years to come? But whatever Fate has in store for you, may Allah the Clement, the Merciful, send peace upon your head, and cast over you the veil of His protection, my little Fatma!

CHAPTER IV.

LEGENDS OF MOSQUES AND MARABOUTS.

The sacred buildings—The Mahommedan clergy—A religion of one belief and six duties—The zaouias—Legends of the mosques in Algiers—Legends of Sidi Abderrahman—The cadi and the slave—Legend of Sidi Bou-Gueddour—The story of the Marabout and the kahouaji—How to distinguish between a true Marabout and an impostor.

ALTHOUGH to the casual observer all the religious buildings of Islam come under the collective heading of "Mosques," they are, in reality, subdivided into the following classes:—

1. The Mosques, *i.e.* buildings for public worship, having a pulpit, or mimbar, whence the oulima intones the prescribed prayers, and addresses counsels to the faithful.

2. The Mesdjid, *i.e.* oratories, which contain no pulpits, and are exclusively reserved for private devotions.

3. The Bit-el-Salad, chapels serving for the sepulture of some saint, or sometimes simply as a place for meditation preparatory to entering the mosque.

All these various buildings are identical in their

construction, and consist of a large vaulted space, supported on columns placed at regular distances. The roof and cupola are usually lined with the graceful pierced stucco-work, and on the walls are frequently panels of tiles bearing inscriptions from the Korán. Candelabra and sconces are affixed, ready for the wax-lights used on great festivals. The floor is covered with prayer-carpets; and it is in order to avoid walking on these sacred fabrics that visitors must remove their shoes. Either just inside the principal entrance or in the outer court is a fountain for the ablutions prescribed before going to prayer.

The head or Supreme Pontiff of all the Mahommedan clergy, "the old man who follows the right way," has his dwelling at Stamboul, and is styled the "Sheikh-el-Islam;" and the chief cleric, or "Sheikh-el-Islam," of every town where Mahommedanism is professed is his vicar. After these follow in the ecclesiastical hierarchy the Imams, the Oulimas, and the Mollahs. There are also the Marabouts, of whom more anon. Finally, amongst the subordinate clergy rank the readers of the Korán, the readers of the Friday prayers, the Aïssouas (or dervishes), and the Santons (monks or fakirs). The two latter classes are fanatics, who subject themselves to tortures and macerations for the glory of

God, and who, when they do not go completely naked, dress themselves in the most singular fashion. The three degrees of the imams, oulimas, and mollahs, might be described as answering in relative importance to our grades of bishops, priests, and deacons; but such comparisons are only approximate, for, in point of fact, the Christian and Mahommedan clergy stand on totally different ground.

The Musulman cleric is merely a man of learning, thoroughly conversant with the writings of the sacred Korán; who, having devoted long nights of reverie and prayer to the interpretation of its text, possesses a clearer insight into the mysteries of religion than is granted to ordinary mortals. Respect and obedience are his due; but he is not looked upon as a *sacerdos* holding any divine mission, and is only a layman specially favoured by Allah. The mueddin (there are two of them attached to each mosque) does not exactly belong to the ranks of the clergy, but is a sort of sacristan, charged with the duty of calling the faithful to prayer.

The Marabouts * are "saints," or holy men revered by the people, who believe them to have the gift of prophecy and the power of working miracles.

---

* The Arabic word is really "Mráb't;" but I have throughout adopted the more euphonious French pronunciation used among Europeans in Algeria, viz. "Marabou."

Their hands and clothes are kissed as they walk along, and they are exempt from all danger of being ill-treated or killed by the populace. When dead, their tombs, their houses, and even any spot where they have prayed, become sacred shrines to be visited devotionally. Their tombs, called *koubbas*, are usually distinguishable by cupolas, which are of white stone, except in the case of a saint who, during his lifetime, had taken and kept inviolably a vow of chastity, in which case the roof of the cupola is of green tiles. Europeans often incorrectly call these koubbas " Marabouts," confounding the tombs themselves with their occupants. Strange to say, madmen and persons of weak intellect are believed to be subject to some divine " possession," and are accordingly revered as Marabouts, so that the most afflicted fool and the most saintly worker of miracles share the same glory.

A detailed account of Islamism, with its numerous religious orders and its various schismatical sects, would not come within the scope of this book; but the tenets of the religion may be briefly epitomized as consisting of one belief and six duties—the former, " There is no God but God, and Mahommed is His Prophet:" the latter, 1, Study of the Korán; 2, Prayer; 3, Ceremonial Ablutions; 4, Fasting; 5, Pilgrimage; and 6, Almsgiving.

The Korán, besides containing the whole code of laws, civil and religious, and thus forming their rule of life, is also remarkable as being the most perfect example of the pure vowelled Arabic of literature,* as distinguished from the corrupt and much simplified speech of later generations. It is indeed due to the intact preservation of the Korán and works contemporary with it that the original language which is thus as it were crystallized within their covers, is still available for students, though not now used colloquially. The universities devoted to the study of the Korán have greatly assisted its preservation. These universities, or *zaouias*, are semi-monastical, semi-educational establishments, serving as places for meditation and religious study. In them the *táleb*, or reader of the Korán (plural *tolba*), writes out sacred amulets to chase away demons and aid the desires of mortals; and from them he is summoned to recite the prescribed passages beside the death-beds of the faithful. In them also study the Arab doctors, astrologers, and cadis. To them pious pilgrims repair for refreshment and alms to help them on their way; so that they serve at once as schools,

---

* For the difference between the conjugation of a verb in the Arabic of literature and the conjugation of the same in the " vulgar tongue," see Appendix B.

places of prayer, and houses where pious hospitality is practised.

Prayer must be made five times a day—at dawn, midday, in the afternoon, at sunset, and at night—the worshippers being turned towards Mecca. The "prayers," so called, consist in reciting in monotone certain verses from the Korán. These may be said in private except on Fridays, when public worship at noon in the mosques is obligatory.

Prayer must always be preceded by ablution, but where water is unobtainable, as with the wandering Arabs of the desert, it suffices for them to pour earth over themselves, with the accustomed gestures.

Pilgrimage to Mecca is of obligation for rich men only; women and the poor being dispensed. Rich ladies often make the pilgrimage, however, and are thenceforward greatly revered for their piety. Eight pilgrimages to Kerouan, the Holy City of North Africa, equal one to Mecca. Amongst the ceremonies performed by the pilgrims during their sojourn at Mecca is the kissing of the stone supposed to have been placed by Adam on the earth, and to have been originally white, but now black owing to the sins of mankind. They must also drink from the spring Zemzem, which gushed out at the command of the angel Gabriel for Hagar and Ishmael when they were on the point of perishing from thirst near the Holy City. They conclude by "stoning the devil," *i.e.* every pilgrim throws seven stones in memory of Abraham, for tradition says that on this spot the patriarch with stones repulsed Sheitan, who would have tempted him to disobey God by refusing to sacrifice Ishmael.* Those who have made the pilgrimage have the right to affix *Hadji* (pilgrim) to their name, and may generally be known by the black rosaries they wear.

Fasting is twofold, voluntary and obligatory. The latter fast commences annually with the new moon in the month of Ramadan.

Great stress is laid on almsgiving amongst the M'sl'mīn. "Almsgiving," says Sidi Mahommed Moul-el-Gendouz, "shuts the seventy doors of evil, and gives passage over Sirath, the bridge sharp as a sword, which stretches between hell and Paradise. God grants mercy only to the merciful. Give alms therefore, were it only the half of a date." And says the Imam Essiyouthi, "Every M'sl'm who clothes a naked M'sl'm, shall in the next world be clothed of Allah in the green vesture of Paradise."

A belief in the unseen world is ever present with

---

* According to the Korán, instead of *Isaac*, as in the Jewish Scriptures.

them. When an ass brays, it is a sign, they say, that the Evil One is passing by; and when a hen clucks, you should recommend yourself to the mercy of Allah, for the hen has seen an angel. Their religious commentaries are full of these fanciful maxims and traditions; as, for example, " When one of you after sneezing says, ' Praise be to God!' the angels reply to him, ' Master of the worlds!' and if he who sneezed has said, ' Master of the worlds!' the angels will respond, ' May He have mercy upon thee!'" "When the sun sets, make haste to hide your children, for at that moment the demons spread themselves over the earth." "When the meat is served, place the dish in the midst, and yourselves round it, that the benediction of Heaven may descend upon you." "When a fly falls into your drinking bowl, immerse it entirely and then draw it out; for in one of its wings there lies evil, and in the other the remedy." "It is a good action to help a man who is without credit, to obtain what he needs. Allah, at the last day, will strengthen upon Sirath the steps of him who has prevailed with a sultan to grant the desires of this man." *

Cool and vast and reposeful is a Mahommedan mosque, with its shady court and plashing fountains,

---

* From the " Djmâa ess'-rin " of the Imam Abderrahman-Djellal-Eddin-Es-siyouthi.

its strewn carpets lying Mecca-wards, and its rigid rows of pillars meeting in fretted horse-shoe arches; a happy retreat for the prayerful believer, and even for the "infidel" traveller a welcome refuge from the scorching sun of Africa. Washington Irving says of them, "The architecture of these mosques was a mixture of Greek and Persian, and gave rise to the Saracenic style, of which Waled may be said to be founder. The slender and graceful palm tree may have served as a model for its columns, as the clustering trees and umbrageous forests of the north are thought to have thrown their massive forms and shadowy glooms into Gothic architecture." * As the hours consecrated to Allah approach, the white flag waves from the minaret and the call to prayer resounds; the bronzed legs splash in the tiled fountain, and the worshippers prostrate themselves till their foreheads touch the ground, while droning voices intone the "F'tah.".

In Algiers, in the days of old, there were no less than twenty-three great mosques; but now, the majority having been destroyed by the conquering French, who dreaded the influence of the fanatical teachers they harboured, there remain only four of importance—the Djemaâ el Djedid, Djemaâ el K'bir,

---

* "Lives of the Successors of Mahomet," by Washington Irving, chap. lvii.

Djemaâ el Saphir, and Djemaâ Sidi Abderrahman—together with a few inferior religious buildings.

The Djemaâ el Djedid (which signifies the New Mosque) is the first to strike one's eye on landing. It dates from A.D. 1660, and though the minaret has been restored and exhibits the incongruity of a modern clock with European figures,* the remainder has been practically untouched. From its position in the Place du Government, and the fact that it is uncarpeted full halfway up its "nave," so that shoes need not be taken off at the entrance, it is the mosque most easy of access to travellers. Its solemnity and its vast shadowy interior surmounted by a grand central dome, strike one as having some of the familiar aspect of a church, and the resemblance is heightened by its cruciform aisles. Saint-Lager, in his "Guide," † accounts for this fact thus: " La légende veut qu'elle ait eu pour architecte un Chrétien qui aurait été empalé quand on s'aperçut de son méfait. Ce qui donne quelque vraisemblance à cette tradition, c'est que son style n'a rien d'Arabe. L'intérieur, avec ses arcades pleincintre et sa voûte en berceau, rappelle en petit Saint-Pierre de Rome.

---

* I have never understood why our figures 1, 2, 3, etc., should be dubbed "Arabic" in contradistinction to the Roman numerals. As a matter of fact, the numeric signs in Arabic are actually these, ١ ٢ ٣ ٤ ٥ ٦ ٧ ٨ ٩ ١٠.

† "Guide Saint-Lager, Alger et ses Environs," p. 57.

L'ensemble est assez monumental." An Arab once told me a pretty story connected with this mosque. It seems that during the Turkish occupation some of the officials who lived in this quarter of the town, were wont to pay their devotions here, surrounded by a body-guard of forty Turkish janissaries. Their rule being most unpopular, the Arabs were constantly plotting insurrections. In one of these attempted risings, it was planned that a large number of Arabs should enter the mosque by stealth, to surprise and kill the Turks and their forty soldiers, who would of course all be absorbed in prayer. Now, in those days, the Turks, fearing treachery, had passed a law forbidding their compatriots to marry Arab women; but one of the forty soldiers had broken this law, and had secretly espoused a beautiful Mauresque in the town. This woman becoming aware of the plot which her countrymen had hatched, and fearful for her husband's life, warned him of what was meditated. He, on his part, then discovered the plot to his masters, with the result that when the Arabs arrived at the mosque, they found only twenty of the soldiers praying, while the remaining twenty stood on guard surrounding them. The Arabs, seeing their plan frustrated, fled, and the massacre was thus averted. On being pressed to disclose how he had heard of the plot, the Turkish soldier at last avowed that he owed the news to his contraband Arab wife. In gratitude for her timely fidelity the law was repealed, and from that time such intermarriages were frequent in Algiers. There is a fine illuminated manuscript Korán, once presented by a sultan to a dey of Algiers, kept here.

The Djemaâ Saphir, in the Rue Kleber, has a curious mimbar, topped with a high wooden pinnacle, and is said to have been built by a pious lady named Saïda, who was of the family of the Prophet.

The Djemaâ el K'bir (*i.e.* the "Great" mosque) is very spacious, very magnificent architecturally, but very cold-looking, as it is devoid of ornament in the interior. The outer court, however, is beautiful, with its grand canopied fountain, and its fig trees and orange trees standing like sentinels. It was built early in the eleventh century A.D.; the minaret, which took six months to construct, being added by Abou-Rachfin, Sultan of Tlemçen, in 1322. The Malekite rite is practised in it.

But the gem of all is the glorious Djemaâ of Sidi Abderrahman. Crowning a hill, it overlooks the shady groves of the Jardin Marengo: and itself covers in all, with its cemetery and outbuildings, a large area of ground intersected by steeply descending paths. This is the most deeply venerated shrine in the whole of Algiers; built, as it was, in 1471 to enclose the remains of the beloved saint Sidi Abderrahman-el-Tslabi, from whom it derives its name.

Since the French conquest, the Arabs have found it impossible to exclude Christians from the mosques here; but to mark the special sanctity of this one, it is only open to Europeans on certain days in the week, artists are forbidden to sketch the interior, and obedience to the rule of unshod feet is rigorously exacted. But what a dream it is! To enter the mosque proper, you pass through a low door, and hastening under the black looks of the attendant to divest yourself of your shoes, you penetrate into a low but splendid hall. Only a "dim religious light" prevails here; but perhaps it enhances—if that were possible—the glories of the fretted tombs surrounded with pliant banners and hung with brocades from the looms of Damascus. The wall-spaces blossom like gardens into parterres of lustred tiles in every conceivable design and colour, and if the El K'bir mosque chills us by its puritanical bareness, here, at least, reigns all the magnificence of a palace in the "Arabian Nights." From every arch hang ex-votos in the shape of costly ostrich eggs, in thin fringed bags of silken network. Other votive offerings, such as massive candles, embroidered hangings, illuminated inscriptions from the Korán, and the like, line the walls in profuse splendour. From the gilded and painted roof droop antique Venetian-glass lustres, which may once have been—who knows?—imported at vast expense from Europe, or captured, likelier still, with more valuable plunder, human or otherwise, by some Corsair captain, and which still reflect prismatic glories over the shrine of Sidi Abderrahman.

Beneath this roof are interred none but great saints or mighty princes. No common dead may lie here. Under that silken-covered sarcophagus rests poor Ahmed, Bey of Constantine, who, defeated and dethroned by the French, died at Algiers. Here are pashas, sheikhs, deys, and countless illustrious priests and princes, and the roll of them is obscured by the mists of antiquity.

A number of women have come to venerate the tombs. Crouching down on the ground beside them, they lift their veils and press their lips to the sarcophagi, to the palls which adorn them, to the banners which droop over them. Who knows what wishes the prayers of the Marabouts lying there may obtain for them? A rich husband for this black-eyed maiden, a child for that girl-wife? But down go the face-veils as we approach, and away they scamper like startled deer.

Passing from this house of tombs through a side arch, we gain the mosque proper, or place of prayer. This is still lower, darker, and more silent, though here the thick Persian carpets have given place to many-coloured tiles, and the pendant ornaments to rows of solemn arches. Off this is the imam's study, with shelves filled full of commentaries and other theological works; and further on again is his dwelling-house. The mosque, which stands in the midst of a crowded Arab cemetery, boasts of more than one beautiful fountain. The great koubba, where the tutelar saint himself reposes in solitary grandeur, stands without in the grounds, a little higher than the main buildings. This, which was also richly carpeted and contained many fine offerings, was crowded with devotees, chiefly women.

We were next led through winding passages, with small oratories and koubbas opening out of them, into a series of outhouses, fitted with ovens, water-supply, and cooking utensils, all on an extensive scale. I had never seen any such arrangement in a mosque before, and was struck with the singularity of it. My husband and our friend Count D——, who was with us, insisted that it must be connected with some animal sacrifice. I, knowing that the ordinary Moslem rite contains no such ceremony,* questioned the imam's son, who had kindly volunteered to act as our guide, but could elicit nothing from him save that the poor of the congregation were fed here with kouss-kouss every Friday. On asking why this mosque alone should afford such lavish hospitality, he would vouchsafe no further information, for a bigoted Musulman hates to be questioned about religious matters, and will often pretend ignorance or deliberately mislead you rather than explain the simplest thing. Long weeks afterwards I learnt from my friend Mahommed ben Hussein Cherif—to whom you were introduced in the previous chapter—the legend on which this custom rests; and as it is sufficiently curious, I will repeat it here.

Some years after the French conquest of Algiers, and when the Jardin Marengo was about to be laid out, instead of planning it where it now is, immediately below the mosque, it was at first proposed that it should replace that building, which was to be demolished for the purpose. The Arabs of course murmured at the thought of such sacrilege, but their conquerors paid little heed to their discontent. One night, however, when the general,

---

* Animals are, however, sacrificed by the pilgrims at the tomb of the Prophet. See Sir R. Burton, "A Personal Narrative of a Pilgrimage to Al-Madinah and Meccah."

MOSQUE OF SIDI ABDERRAHMAN.

who at that time acted as governor, was in bed, he woke suddenly, and, petrified with terror, saw a huge serpent, which glided forward and with one spring coiled itself round his throat. While the trembling governor lay expecting to feel at every moment the fatal fang which would put an end to his days on earth, the serpent—who was indeed no ordinary snake—hissed out in Arabic these words: "Dost thou not know me, general? I am the Sidi Abderrahman, and thou hast designed to demolish my mosque and shrine; and behold, I have come hither to slay thee." The wretched man implored forgiveness, and swore if his life were spared, that the shrine should be sacred for ever, and none should lay a finger on it. At length the sidi consented to pardon him on condition that he should present himself before the imam of the mosque, and perform whatever that functionary should command. Accordingly the next morning, at break of day, the still-terrified general hastened tremblingly to the mosque, and related how the Sidi Abderrahman had appeared to him in the form of a serpent in the night, together with all that had passed between them. The imam, after sternly rebuking him for his meditated sacrilege, ordained that as the saint had consented to pardon him, he should thenceforth show his gratitude by providing an annual fund sufficient to feed all the poor of the community with kouss-kouss every Friday. The general, glad to be let off so easily, readily acceded; the garden was laid out lower down the hill, the endowment was made, and the weekly feast of kouss-kouss is still provided for the hungry poor.

Around the memories of all their great men and holy places are clustered numbers of such miracle-tales, beloved of the Arabs, whose appetite for the marvellous is simply insatiable. Whether in the case of the particular one just narrated there might be some grain of truth on which the fable has been built up, some dim tradition of a proposed demolition of their mosque, resented by the imams, and abandoned in consequence by the authorities, I cannot say. But the present generation believe in it firmly; and no doubt the tale of the governor's discomfiture serves as a partial solace to their wounded pride, when they see the foot of the stranger defiling their sacred ground.

Another curious legend in connection with the same mosque is as follows. There was once a cadi of El Djzaïr who had a favourite slave. This slave was falsely accused by a cruel Turk (for it was during the Turkish occupation of Algiers) of having penetrated to the apartments of his (the Turk's) wives, and stolen therefrom a valuable bracelet.

The cadi accordingly caused his slave's hands to be cut off, and banished him from his presence. But soon afterwards the slave's innocence was proved; for the bracelet was found on a window-ledge in the harem.

The cadi, hearing this, sent messengers to seek for his slave, who was found by them with both his hands miraculously restored; for the slave was a Marabout, though none had known it until then. When he came into the presence of his old master the cadi asked his pardon for having, through ignorance, caused him to be unjustly punished. But the slave refused to pardon him; wherefore Allah put away the cadi, so that he could nowhere be found, and no man knew what had become of him. After fifteen years the slave-Marabout relented, and he forgave the cadi, and set forth to find him and fetch him back to his native city; and, being miraculously instructed of Allah, found him in Stamboul, and together they returned to El Djzaïr, and together are buried beneath the same cupola in the mosque of Sidi Abderrahman.

Further to the right, in the Arab town, and completely enclosed by houses, is the Zaouia of Sidi Bou-Gueddor, who, needless to say, has also his legend. One day, while toiling through the roughly paved streets, we came suddenly upon a mysterious little green door, before which tall painted tapers were blinking; and I inquired of our escort, "Īa Mahommed ben Hussein, what is that little green door; and why are there candles burning before it?" And he answered, "That, *ia lalla* (O lady), was the door of the house of Sidi Bou-Gueddor, who lived some three centuries ago, and was a mighty Marabout. Once, when the Spaniards sent forth ships to try and take El Djzaïr, the people ran up to his house here in haste to tell him that the bay was full of Spanish ships. Now Sidi Bou-Gueddor was a potter, and made earthen vessels. He went straightway down through the streets of the town, carrying with him only his staff and some of the earthen pots which he had made, till he came to the edge of the sea. And he beheld the bay full of the accursed Spanish ships. And he lifted up his stick and smote the sea with it, so that it became stormy, and the Spanish galleons were driven further and further back from the coast. And he cast down his earthen pots upon the shore and broke them, and at every pot that he broke a vessel sank. So he saved the town from the Spaniards, and ever since we account his house holy as a mosque; and on every 'day of prayer' we burn candles there, as thou seest, for he was a great Marabout."

That the credulity of the Arabs as regards the miraculous powers of their saints extends even to the Marabouts of the present day, will be evinced by the following anecdote.

A notable saint, who lately died at Blidah, having cause for anger against a kahouaji there, entered his café and broke in pieces a clock which hung on the wall. The kahouaji promptly appealed to the French Commissaire de Police; but when this functionary had put the Marabout in prison for destroying his neighbour's goods, to the astonishment of the bystanders the holy man was observed escaping through the wall on the opposite side, although there was no visible aperture for the purpose. Once free, he returned to the café and miraculously restored the broken pieces of the clock to their places, so that it was as good as ever. Wherefore the people of Blidah perceived that the finger of Allah had touched this man, and thenceforward he was venerated as a Marabout whilst he lived, and when he died, not long ago, his tomb became a holy place.

Hundreds of such tales might be collected in Algeria alone; but the narratives given above (as also some respecting Tunisian saints, which I shall come to further on) have never, I think, as yet appeared in print, and will serve as fair specimens of their kind. As for their veracity, they were related to me in all seriousness by Mahommed ben Hussein Cherif, and other equally solemn personages who certainly believed in them firmly; and, as was only polite on my part, I hearkened and wrote them down with an equally grave countenance.

After all, if one comes to think of it, are the miracles of these Marabouts any whit more astonishing to the common-sense mind than the winking virgins of mediæval Christianity, or the still-continuing alleged liquefaction of the blood of St. Januarius at Naples, about which, you will remember, poor Charles Ravenshoe used to tease Father Mackworth?

On inquiring whether there were ever such things as impostors among the numbers of these wonder-working saints, I ascertained that in the good old times, before the trail of the Frenchman was over them all, a man claiming to be a Marabout without being able to show just cause for his claim was cast by the other Marabouts into a fiery furnace. If he came out alive, all further doubts were, of course, removed. As to those who did *not* come out alive, *tant pis pour eux!*

And these things were told unto me by Mahommed, the son of Hussein.

CHAPTER V.

THE ENVIRONS OF ALGIERS.

Le Chateau d'H———.—The story of Ali Agha and the " Peeping Tom " of Birmandreis—The tombs at Bou-Zareah—A Kabyle village—The sands at Maddrab—The Corsairs' Creek—The " Fort des Revenants "—A soldier degraded—A modern mosque—The Algerian diligences—Hammam Melouan—Amongst the Kabyles of the Atlas Mountains.

A GLORIOUS day in January, as January days can be in Algeria—warm sunshine, a clear sky, and nothing to do. How spend the time better than by accepting the invitation which lies beside us to *déjeuner* at a château about seven kilomètres from the town, proceeding afterwards to explore the old tombs at Bou-Zareah?

A beautiful drive up winding hill-roads and through the pretty little village of Birmandreis (which, being translated, means the well of Captain Mourad = *Bir Mourad reïs*), brings us to our destination, the grounds of the Château d'H———, where a cheery English host and hostess dispense their kindly hospitality. This is one of several splendid

Moorish villas which, vacated at the conquest by their original owners, have been snapped up by English pioneers while the colony was yet in its infancy. They saw, with the discrimination of their race, the advantage of securing homes which combined those luxuries of glorious climate, fertile soil, and fairy-like architecture, that make of an Algerian *terrain* an earthly paradise; and have long been settled, literally "under the shadow of their own vine and fig tree," in those white-roofed palaces which dot the slopes of Mustafa. This particular one was once the summer resort of the cruel Turk Ali Agha, who was deservedly massacred by the Arabs, and who is supposed to have left a vast treasure concealed here.

Through an outer court, with central fountain and walls aflame with orange bignonia, we pass along a cloister-like corridor upheld on ancient columns, and so to the superb inner court, now glassed over and used as a morning room. Here may be seen a double tier of Moorish arches, relieved by the foliage of creeping plants, which are suspended in brackets from their capitals. Soft divans, carpets and cushions galore, and a profusion of flowers and photographs make up a most "lived-in" interior. Everywhere one enjoys the rare satisfaction of finding European comfort grafted on to Saracenic splendour. The latest London "Society" journal lies open beside a jar of antique Kabyle pottery; and on a carpet that may have come from the weavers of Kerouan a beautiful French poodle and an all but human dachshund condescend to go through their lessons for our gratification. But although every modern comfort is to be found here, it exists in an unobtrusive undercurrent, and not a note jars on one's eye. There is cause for thankfulness here to an artistic soul; for such a house might have fallen into the hands of the Goths and Vandals, who would have razed it to the ground and substituted a neat villa residence, with a hall-door in the middle, and bow-windows on either side. Or, worse still, it might have become the property of some Philistine, who, while leaving the actual structure intact, would have furnished the interior in "suites" of black and gold, upholstered with the latest cretonne. Upon little tables are heaped huge dishes of various fruits belonging to the orange tribe, of all shapes and sizes, from cedras to mandarines; of all shades, from palest lemon to reddest flame; and wonderfully well do they relieve the dark woodwork of the balustrade. From a drawing-room opening off the upper gallery stretches a wide view over this African Garden of Eden; and let into the walls are old tiles arranged in panels, which at a distance might be taken for the finest

Persian hangings, so well blended are colour and pattern. It is impossible to give an idea of the mellow beauty of these ancient ceramics when so displayed. Our hostess tells us they were all picked out of the floors of distant rooms where they blushed unseen, and with admirable taste she formed the plan of filling in her wall-panels with them.

After *déjeuner*, which concludes with golden home-grown dates that melt like honey in the mouth, and are very unlike the mummified brown objects retailed by fruiterers in England, we adjourn for coffee, chartreuse, and cigarettes to the adjacent library. This overlooks the old harem garden, more grimly walled round than was ever the pleasaunce of cloistered nuns. But if it be true that "stone walls do not a prison make," perhaps the ladies of old, who knew of no happier existence, may have dallied peacefully enough beneath the rose trees here. And this brings me to a curious legend connected with the château, too characteristic of its former owner to be omitted. While strolling about the shady grounds after *déjeuner*, we came upon a huge tank, which I should roughly guess to be about forty feet by twenty. This tank, fringed with the miniature white and mauve wild irises (the veritable heraldic fleur-de-lys), common in the woods here, was once the bathing-place for the wives of the redoubtable Ali Agha. Our hostess pointed out first the approach by which the ladies came to it from the harem, and secondly, a tall tree having one of its branches bent and withered; and thereby hangs the tale.

Half the area of the tank was once roofed over, in order that the fair bathers might idle there, letting the cool water lap their ivory limbs, without fear of observation from without. But one day a wicked interloper, a "Peeping Tom," not of Coventry, but of Birmandreis, crept softly over the ground and climbed up into the great tree that still overhangs the tank, to feast his envious eyes. One of the women looking up suddenly, saw him, and, with shrieks, she and her companions, gathering up their gauzy draperies, robed themselves and fled; for well they knew that to be caught submitting to the gaze of any man but their lord meant for them the bowstring. So they sent to tell Ali, and the first question he put was, "Where was this man hidden?" And when they told him, "In the tree which hangs over the water's edge," Ali replied, "Then from that tree shall he be hanged." So the guards went forth and scoured the country round till they overtook the man, and he was brought before Ali. And he was hanged by the neck from a branch of that tree, as Ali commanded, till the branch bowed down beneath his weight. And because on it so accursed a traitor had met his just doom, the branch has never borne leaf since, though the parent tree lives and flourishes. So runs the legend, and *I, moi qui vous parle,* have seen that branch, and it is bent and withered still!

But the afternoon wears on, and we must away to Bou-Zareah. The road which passes El Biar (*i.e.* the wells) is lined with the various wild flowers which grace this land—trails of clematis with greeny-white blossoms, a trefoil with wide-open yellow stars, a dignified member of the lily tribe from whose spreading leaves springs a beautiful tall spike of clustered white flowers, pink and brown fly orchids, giant hemlock, and a host of other beauties. Here and there along the road come strings of donkeys, carrying sand in baskets of green rushes, and pursued by the objurgations of brown-skinned drivers in tattered gandouras.

Here we come at last to the tombs, which stand in a wild garden laid out by the hand of Nature alone; and Nature in Northern Africa requires no gardener to help her. Palm trees, which from the width of their stems must be very old, though the winds of many winters howling round their height have dwarfed them; aloes, with edges sharply toothed; clumps of prickly pear; and underneath all, peeping quietly up in shady corners, roots of

ARAB GRAVES AT BOU-ZAREAH.

cyclamen, which at present show only their round and spotted leaves, but which later on will blush with rosy blossoms. And here, there, and everywhere, on this savage parterre, white koubbas spring up like gigantic mushrooms, and little low graves inflate the grassy grounds. A koubba is a queer construction, and these are very old. Stooping, you enter, by a low opening, into a small, circular domed building, with just room for about three people to stand upright around the *catafalque*. The body really lies in the ground below the centre of the building; but when the earth has closed over it, a bier is placed immediately over the spot, and on that bier rests an empty coffin draped with what hangings the friends of the deceased can afford. Sometimes lamps and candles are lit in the mausoleum on Fridays and festivals. Koubbas usually contain only the bodies of saints or great men; the graves of the common herd being made like ours, sometimes surrounded with coloured tiles, and having headstones covered with Arabic inscriptions. The headstones on the men's graves are usually distinguished by terminating in turban-shaped heads. The bodies of the dead are simply wrapped in clothes, and laid in the ground with their faces turned towards Mecca. According to the Moslem dogma, the soul does not quit the body until after the latter has been for some hours interred, when the angel Gabriel is believed to come and judge it, after which, if the dead person has died with the profession of faith upon his lips—"There is one God, and Mahommed is His Prophet," his sins are pardoned, and his soul soars to Paradise, with its cool fruits, its green vestures, and its seductive houris. The women visit the cemeteries on Fridays in large numbers, and pray at the tombs.

A drive of about half a mile further brings us to a curious hill village, with an encampment of Kabyles. From the road nothing is visible but a forest of prickly pear immensely thick and high; but on looking about for an opening, we find a tiny path between the bushes and follow it, keeping discreetly in the middle, for the sharp thorns of these *figues de Barbarie* are not pleasant to tackle at close quarters. A few paces more, and we become aware of little low rude huts of rough stones, innocent of mortar, and roofed with branches and a very rough imitation of thatch. Each hut is surrounded by its own prickly-pear hedge, and seems a fitting abode for members of a barbarous tribe. For these Kabyles, the descendants of the ancient Berbers, are nothing but savages—the men clad in dark striped gandouras, the women unveiled; and houses and people alike present an extraordinary contrast to the highly civilized Arabs, with whom they have nothing in common but the religion once forced upon them by their conquerors. The barbarians jabber kindly at us in their queer tongue (of which, needless to say, we understand not one word) and invite us by gestures into their dark and dirty shanties; but a very brief survey of these suffices, and after bestowing largess, while we narrowly escape walking over a crowd of errant babies and hens, we regain the high-road.

After pausing on the top of the grand hill of Bou-Zareah to enjoy the view below, we pursue our way, alighting *en route* at the Church of Notre Dame d'Afrique, which boasts a black Virgin and a solid silver St. Michael, besides many quaint ex-votos from sailors, and bears on an arch over the high altar the touching inscription, "Notre Dame d'Afrique, priez pour nous et pour les Musulmans." From thence down homewards through the shady groves of the Vallée des Consuls, so named because in the time of the deys the various European consuls had their residences out here, feeling probably more secure in thus forming a suburban group than if they had been scattered through the town in the very jaws of the "unspeakable Turk." *

* Even here they were not safe. Lane-Poole says, "Heavy bribes— called 'the customary presents'—had to be distributed on the arrival

As these sketches do not presume to encroach upon the functions of a guide-book, I purposely omit all mention of such obvious resorts as the Ravin de la Femme Sauvage, the Jardin d'Essai, etc., which those useful works—there are several of them devoted to Algeria—will point out to the traveller. Somehow, though I own it seems ungrateful and even presumptuous, I always resent the way in which a guide-book conveys information. It has an irritating trick of "dotting your i's" for you, and showing you dissected details of what you are to admire before you have had time to grasp the gorgeous whole. It leads you up to the portal of some historic city, to reach which has been your life's dream, and, allowing you no time to interweave the contrasting webs of romance and reality, it dashes flippantly through a brief *résumé* of several centuries, and in the same breath confronts you with such dry modern statistics as these: "*Population*, —000; *square mileage*, so and so; *water supply*, from such and such a reservoir; *places of worship*, —."

---

of each fresh consul. . . . The Government presents were never rich enough, and the unlucky consul had to make up the deficit out of his own pocket. The dey would contemptuously hand over a magnificently jewelled watch to his head cook in the presence of the donor. . . . The presence of a remonstrating admiral in the bay was a new source of danger; for the consul would probably be thrown into prison, and his family turned homeless into the streets, while his dragoman received a thousand stripes of the bastinado."—"The Barbary Corsairs," p. 263.

And there my pen fails me; for where, outside the pages of guide-books and directories, will you find enumerated such an astounding variety of sects? I actually saw lately, in an Anglo-Italian paper devoted to the interests of English tourists, the address and hours of service of the "Christian Apostolic Church of Rome," in a certain city! I bewonder me (as the German phrase hath it) what, in the name of all that's holy, the Christian Apostolic Church of Rome may be?

No; I can humbly try to convey an idea of the Moors and their manners, as they struck my admiring eyes; but if you want to know the extent of the governor's summer palace, the exact height of the Colonne Voirol, or how many indiarubber trees there are in the grand avenue of the Jardin d'Essai, together with the precise classification of the inhabitants into "Jews, Turks, Infidels, and heretics," I must refer you to our old friend, the guide-book. For me the unaccustomed paths have more charm than the stock excursions of personally conducted caravans.

It was in one of our endeavours to escape from the beaten track that we lighted upon a beautiful little bay near the village of Maddrab. I don't think it has a name. It is not apparently given in the maps, and, excepting one deserted cottage, there is nothing to be seen save sea and sky, and a long track of sand strewn with, oh, such shells! The delicate Venus's ear lies here, lobe upwards, displaying its little pierced holes and its sheeny mother-of-pearl surface glistening with rainbow hues. And turritellas and bullas and cowries are here, too, in countless varieties, "spotted and straked," with the thorny sea-urchin and the white cuttle-fish. I wandered on and on over the trackless sand, gathering up the treasures which the blue Mediterranean wafted to my feet, till a sudden barrier of rocks arose and daunted me. Round a further bend lies Sidi Ferruch, where the French effected their landing; and inland, on the left, the road runs to Staoueli and La Trappe, the living grave of the monks who never speak. Retracing our way, a drive of about an hour and a half back along the Kolea road to Point de Pescade, brought us to a little wayside restaurant and lunch. And after lunch, following a steep track up an arid hill, we plunged into a deserted Turkish fortress, which frowned down upon the rocky shore of the Crique des Corsairs, lying at its foot. The ruin is in a perfect state of preservation, and seems to be built on much the same plan as our own feudal castles. In high glee we climbed by corkscrew stairs to the highest tower, clambered and slid down into the lowest dungeons, and threw stones into the deep well which must have supplied the garrison with water. Wild mignonette has found a foothold on those steep walls now, and the grass all around is peacefully blue with wild irises. But the name of the bay below has its own grim significance, and, if it be true, as gossip says, that the French call it " Le Fort des Revenants," and will not go near it at night, it is easy enough to people it in imagination with the appropriate shades of unhappy captives who may have been dragged up to it over those steep rocks by the Corsairs of old.

From this point onwards to St. Eugène the drive is flat and uninteresting. There are no Moorish antiquities, and the road is bordered at intervals by desolate, incomplete-looking villas and lonely hamlets built by Spanish fishermen; for this is a quarter almost entirely colonized by Spaniards. It looks as if the votaries of a building craze had once made this part of the coast their own; but some panic must have suddenly seized the contractors, and the shrines of the jerry-building god remain, many of them unfinished, and most of them empty, and all equally ugly with their brick walls, vivid green *persiennes*, and half-laid-out gardens. On abandoned hoardings stretches a vast and inappropriate waste of advertisements, in which " Chocolat Menier" predominates with "byrrh." This latter, like "that blessed word Mesopotamia," must surely have some soothing influence on the vulgar mind, so persistently does it recur on French kiosks and bathing-machines. *Les colons* reign supreme here, *les indigènes* being rarely met with. All is dreary, and the only excitement is when a diligence pulls up at some wayside *brasserie*, and the well-to-do passenger from the *coupé* descends to indulge in a vermout and seltzer, while the poor Arab travellers huddle closer together in their covered roost on the top of the vehicle.

But as we approach the faubourg of St. Eugène the scene becomes more cheerful, the houses more closely grouped. St. Eugène is a lively suburb, many rich Jews having their villas there, and the gardens are bright with flowers. Beyond it lie the French and Jewish cemeteries; and to the gate of the latter are affixed some curious police regulations, rendered necessary by the habits of Hebrew mourners, such as "All loud cries and demonstrative gestures are prohibited."

We reached Algiers at last, late in the afternoon, by the Bab-el-Oued, or "Gate of the River," and I remember witnessing a sad sight as we drove through the lower end of the town. On passing the military prison (once a Turkish fort) we saw a large crowd gathering, and on inquiry found that a Zouave soldier was to be degraded and imprisoned for insubordination towards an officer. In a few minutes a detachment of Zouaves marched up and formed a square in front of the prison. Some of the Chasseurs d'Afrique and of the *génie* quartered at Algiers were also present. When the troops were drawn up in order, two sergeants were despatched into the prison to fetch the offender, who emerged bareheaded in their custody, and was marched into position in the middle of the square. His commanding officer advanced, read out a long document to him (which was quite inaudible to us in the distance), and then gave the word of command, " Coupez-lui les boutons ! " The buttons were then hacked off his tunic and fell to the ground. The prisoner was marched three times slowly round the square under the gaze of his comrades' eyes, and then the drums of the Zouave band sounded a hoarse rattle, drumming him out of the regiment he had so disgraced, and the culprit was led back into the prison, the great door of which will open no more to him for many a long day. It was a melancholy sight ; but one would have felt sorrier for the poor wretch had he not had such a bad countenance, and worn such a hardened, sullen expression. He was a Spaniard, for all the Spanish and other nationalities who have settled in the colony have to serve their term under the conscription; and with such a mixed multitude to control, the French are forced to maintain strict discipline amongst their troops.

Another wild and interesting expedition which we made was across the Harrach river to Hammam Melouan, where, in a gorge of the Atlas Mountains, hot thermal waters rise, used exclusively by the Arabs and Jews of the district. No railway runs near it, and it took us from nine a.m. till past one, hard driving all the time, to reach it.

The road from Algiers led us first through Kouba and Birkadem. The former is named after the tomb, or *koubba*, of Hadj Pacha (A.D. 1543), which stood where now rise the magnificent church and seminary. Jostling these stands a brand-new mosque, a startling and unexpected sight. Here, in the very heart of Islam, one connects the idea of a mosque with buildings as many centuries old as its creed, with dark wells and shadowy arches, beneath which glide the slipperless worshippers. But this new edifice rears itself with something of the pert smugness of any Baptist "Eleazar" which defies tradition in an English village. I did not enter, but feel convinced that the fountain within is provided with the latest thing in patent taps and plumber's

THE ENVIRONS OF ALGIERS. 113

fittings, and the prayer-carpets hail from Lyons or Kidderminster. As the road winds on, we pass now and then an isolated Arab farmhouse, or the remains of some ancient Roman aqueduct. Later on we traverse the fertile Metidja plain, where acres and acres of vines, in their fresh spring verdure, cover the land. Next comes Sidi Moussa, which, for all its Arabic name, is nothing but a disappointing European village, built by the colonizers, with long streets of two-storied houses, a church, a village green, and an inn or two. In front of one of these the diligence has just pulled up to water the horses. These diligences form quite a feature in Algeria. Traversing large tracts of country where no railway runs, they convey at absurdly low prices a very mixed multitude, consisting of farmers, vine-growers, priests, religious, and those Arabs who, instead of bestriding their asses as of old, prefer to avail themselves of this means of locomotion; not to mention other minute passengers who pay no fares, but doubtless make the journey with every comfort to themselves, if not to their fellow-travellers. The crazy vehicles, which are usually painted bright yellow, and are drawn by three horses abreast, look like lineal descendants of Noah's ark; and to see them lumbering along one would certainly place the date when they emerged from the coach-builder's

I

hands as contemporary with the First Empire, if not earlier. On the body of a high, narrow omnibus is grafted a front compartment, or *coupé*, glazed in; and on a seat overhanging its windows is perched the driver, so that the unfortunate passengers in that post of honour can have little air and less view. On the top of the roof rises a hood-like sloping shanty of white sail-cloth, supported on hoops; and it would be a difficult task to guess how many squatting, crouching Arabs can be packed away in its recesses, together with their *impedimenta* of dirty bundles or sacks full of live hens for the market. How they ever climb up into this pen or down from it I have never fathomed. But houp-la! on they go again, *et vive les diligences de l'Algérie!*

More fertile fields, covered this time with sweet-scented geranium, from which the Trappist monks extract the essence for their perfumes. Then, at thirty kilomètres from Algiers, the little village of Rovigo—and with it the last outpost of civilization—is passed, and the wild Atlas Mountains loom nearer and nearer. On a bleak hillside is a quarry of white cement, and the workmen are passing baskets full of it along an aerial railway to the building where it will be converted into plaster of Paris. All the little figures of praying Arabs, etc., sold in Algiers and Cairo are made from this plaster; but it looked a very lonely spot for the small group of workmen employed there, who rarely exchange words with a living soul save the itinerant natives.

Once we met a group of Arabs leading a poor aged, mangy, and very weary-looking lioness by a chain. They said they were taking her home (after exercise) to the Marabout to whom she belonged; for it is a superstition that Marabouts have power to subdue wild animals, and that lions will come and fawn at their feet; and in order to keep up this delusion, many Marabouts own a tame lion; whence comes the Algerian proverb, "Every lion goes home to his Marabout." They said this one had been found when young in the forests near Oran.

Wilder and wilder grows the scene, as we cross for the first time the great Harrach river, whose bed is bordered by a wide shingly beach. On it are constructed a group of low huts, very roughly set up, with straw roofs supported on poles. These are the habitations of a few poor Arabs who make their livelihood by collecting from the river-bed the stones needed for mending roads. Then through rocky defiles, where we meet an occasional *cortège* of Arabs, evidently *en route* for the Algiers market, for their donkeys are laden with chickens and charcoal (what a sublime opportunity for alliteration !). Their wives follow, sometimes unveiled in these solitary spots, though they hastily cover their faces as we approach. Once the narrow road, bordered with high rocks on one side and with the river foaming below it, gave way to a dell full of wild oleanders already budding. When in flower this must indeed be like a bit of fairyland. After once more crossing the Harrach river, we finally emerge at the foot of that distant Atlas range to which, seeing it daily in the blue distance, it has long been my ambition to penetrate. Magnificent rocks, dotted with prickly pear and wild aloes, rise in sharp lines. "Dans le temps," remarks the driver, there were monkeys here, but of late years they have retreated further up the passes.

And now here at last is Hammam Melouan, and very glad we are to find ourselves at our destination. The village consists of a few Kabyle and Arab huts, the *établissement*, a row of slightly more civilized-looking cabins which the Jews occupy in the bathing season, and one shop. With the help of the guardian genius of the place, a pleasant French-speaking Kabyle, we spread our luncheon under a tree; and after lunch he takes us to explore the *établissement*, if a square shanty full of evil-smelling water could be dignified by

such a name. The water bubbles up everywhere from the ground, yellow and boiling hot, and some of the Algerian Jews, who come here for the thermal season, have little private *cabines*, of which our friend acts as caretaker. He also keeps the shop, which, needless to say, belongs to a Jew, and has to yield strict account of the goods sold there when his patron comes.

He then took us into his hut, where he and his brother, with their respective wives, lived, a *partie carrée*, apparently in perfect harmony. His own wife was ill of a feverish ague, poor thing (for this valley is not free from malarial exhalations at nightfall), and she sat crouched up on her blanket, looking both sick and sorry. The brother's wife had a beautiful old triangular silver ornament, covered with cabalistic inscriptions, hanging round her neck. It is refreshing to meet with the genuine article occasionally nowadays, when the bazaars are full of paltry imitations of native jewellery made in Birmingham to deceive the unwary. This lady was busy making kouss-kouss for the family. They spoke only Kabyle, but we made up for our lack of mutual conversation by smiling sweetly at each other; for these wild people have the kindest hearts in the world.

Somehow or other, by an occult instinct, the

remaining inhabitants of this solitary glen had gathered that strangers were on the spot—an unusual fact, for except the few Jews and Arabs who come in the bathing season, the place is rarely visited. Accordingly, on emerging from our friend's hut they stole up and surrounded us in an admiring group. Our guide greeted the new-comers by touching the palms of each one's hands, they then putting the said palms to their own lips.

Up in a cleft of the rock behind some trees squatted all the women of the party in a circle, with a few babies. They had apparently no occupation of any kind, but looked remarkably cheerful. They were beautifully tattooed in elaborate devices on every visible inch of their persons. When I came upon the scene they were occupied in tickling a baby which lay on the grass in the middle of the circle, and from their attitudes I felt as if I were "cutting in" at a game of hunt-the-slipper. They were every one Kabyles, and knew not a word of Arabic, so that conversation was impossible; but they roared with laughter when I joined in the amusement of tickling the baby. When I rejoined the superior lords of creation below, our friend remarked in French, with a grin, "Eh bien, la femme du Kabyle jolie, hein?"

I asked whether they had a mosque near. They

said, "No; only a little koubba up the hill," to which they conducted us. It was a tiny place, dating "from the time of the Turks," but they could not tell me what saint was buried there. Only it must have been a very sacred spot, for on a thornbush which grew near the entrance hung countless ex-votos in the shape of purses, little bits of rag, etc. It is a far cry from Algeria to Ireland, but I have seen the bushes beside some traditionally holy well there covered by the Roman Catholic peasants with the like ragged offerings and presenting an exactly similar appearance.

After this all the men crowded round us asking if we could oblige them with *lo monnaie de cent sous;* for they were all possessed of five-franc pieces, but small change in this unfrequented valley was evidently at a premium. Fortunately we were able to accommodate a good many. We lent our field-glasses to each in turn, and they were much interested in scanning the distance—all but one superior gentleman in a yellow caftan, who, having travelled as far as Algiers, had seen such instruments before, and thought it was the smart thing to look *blasé.* We pressed the remains of our luncheon on them, but they would only accept *el hroubz* (bread), as the cold fowl had not been slaughtered according to their law. We finished up by standing them all coffee at the kahoua, a simple thatched hut with no light save from the doorway. The kahouaji did not make at all bad coffee, if it had not been spoilt—as most Arab coffee is—by being too sweet.

But, alas! the sun was getting low, and we had a weary drive before us, so the horses had to be put to. We lifted little Mahommed, our guide's son, into the carriage, and he crowed with delight when his father told him in fun that we would take him with us to Algiers. He was a funny little man in a red burnous, only able to talk Kabyle; and the one word of Arabic he could understand was *skr* (sugar), which is the same in both languages. At last we bade farewell to our friends with much regret. Their perfect manners and the way in which, without the slightest self-consciousness, they had done the honours of their lonely glen struck me very much; and among my pleasantest memories of Algeria is the thought of these gentle, simple-hearted, kindly folk. Little Mahommed, his red burnous flying behind him, ran after the carriage as long as his breath held out. Poor little fellow! I fear he had taken our invitation seriously, and would willingly have left his father and mother to come with us. I did not dare to look round for fear of raising false hopes, but until a bend in the road hid the valley completely from our view I heard the little pattering footsteps still following in our wake.

CHAPTER VI.

BLIDAH.

The orange groves—A Hammam—The fire-eaters—An Arab stud—The Gorges de la Chiffa and the Ruisseau des Singes—What France has done for Algeria.

A WEARISOME journey inland in one of the typical Algerian trains which take over two hours to do what they might accomplish in one, brings us to the famous orange plantations of Blidah. In 1830 the whole space between the sea and the Atlas range now traversed by the railway was a morass alive with panthers. Now the malarial marshes have given place to vast woods of carefully cultivated eucalyptus, and the wild fauna to the fruit-laden asses of the colonist. Indeed, so greatly are the ranks of the latter thinned, that though wild boar and monkeys are still plentiful in parts, the panthers and jackals have to be stalked for days by the enthusiastic sportsman, and I question whether ten are shot in a year now. As for Blidah itself it is a place of flowers and fragrance, given up as it is to the cultivation of countless *hectares* of Parma violets and miles of orange trees. I find, on referring to our statistic-loving friend the guide-book, that the exact number of the trees is sixty thousand; and that five to six millions of oranges are annually exported from the town, forming, next to the vines, the greatest source of revenue to the colony. No need of a Hercules *here* to seize this golden fruit; it falls unheeded at one's feet in the beautiful groves, which seem aglow with the profusion of these flame-like spheres.

The old Arab town having been destroyed by earthquake in 1825, was almost entirely re-constructed by the French when they took possession in 1830. Of course, therefore, needless to say, there are the inevitable Parisian arcades and the inevitable grass square railed round and planted with palm trees, which always suggests to me an effort on the part of the French emigrant to produce the pomposity of a *place* suitable to the dignity of the colony, while all the time he is struggling to suppress a reminiscence of his native village green. Every here and there an old doorway or other fragment of antiquity still rears itself amongst the modern constructions, and it was in search of these and other curiosities of the native quarter that we bent

our steps, after a horrible repast of tough meat and
garlic at one of the primitive hotels. The women
are noticeable here, for they only expose the veriest
corner of one eye, the other being tightly shrouded.
The men wear mostly white burnouses. We had
secured an Arab guide, who, without explaining his
intentions, promptly conducted us to the Hammam.
I had not the vaguest idea that we were going to
precipitate ourselves into the moist recesses of a
Turkish bath, and was startled to find myself, ere
I had well crossed the threshold of what I had taken
to be a mosque, plunging ankle deep in hot water!
Before I had recovered, another shock awaited me,
for a gentleman in the very airiest and scantiest of
clothing (he was, it transpired, the shampooer)
fled tumultuously past us to an inner room. The
place was so hot and humid that I lacked courage
to pursue my researches, though during the women's
hours a visit in suitable attire would be interesting,
for the Bain Maure is the great meeting-place for
these secluded beings, where they may throw aside
their *haïcks* and, reclining on the divans, gossip at
their ease. At the exit stood a dear old fat negress,
the mistress of the establishment, whose black face
beamed on us as with pretty native courtesy she
kissed the coins we tendered her.

Our next halt was at a little zaouia where a

séance of the fire-eating Aïssouas was being held. A number of tolba and imams were seated cross-legged on the floor of a long low room, chanting verses from the Korán, in tones singularly like our church "plain-song," accompanying themselves on derboukas. The performing Aïssoua stood in front of them, and our guide posted us in the courtyard on the threshold, where we could see all without obtruding our presence on the assembly, who seemed inclined to scowl at the infidel spectators. After much intoning from the rest, the dervish, who was attired only in a loose white gandoura, began to tremble all over and sway about, while the music waxed louder. Presently he called for fire, and an attendant took up a huge bunch of tow and dried grass, set light to it, and handed it to him. Then began the most extraordinary performance I have ever seen. He held the flaming bundle close to him, making passes with it over his face, under his armpits, and holding it between his skin and his thin garment till it seemed as if either one or other *must* catch fire; but no! not even his hands were scorched. Louder drummed the music, more frantically fast rose the sing-song chants as the flames licked his body and lit up his elfin face, until at last with one wild cry he rammed the fiery mass into his mouth and swallowed, or appeared to swallow it, whole.

Finally, water having been brought to him, he took a deep draught and sank down immediately afterwards in an inert heap on the floor. We were standing close to him all the while, so close that we ourselves could feel the fierce heat of the flames, and were half blinded by the smoke, and one can only say that if it was, as I suppose, a trick, it was a very clever one. Possibly he might have rubbed his skin with some native salve which renders fire harmless, for the Arabs have an ancient and very complete pharmacopœia; but I should be very sorry to try and emulate the performance. The people draw auguries from the performances of these Aïssouas, who are also soothsayers.

After a visit to the Café Maure of Sidi Brahim Rabbash, where the usual dancing girls performed to the strains of the usual native orchestra, we walked home through the moonlight. Ah, what superb moonlight shines on these Arab towns! Never have I seen such effulgence as there. When their beautiful courts and arches are bathed in that soft flood, one feels it no wonder that the old pagan Bedawys, " the Arabs of the Ignorance," used to worship " the three moon-goddesses," * until

---

* " El Lāt, the bright moon; Menāh, the dark; and El 'Uzzá, the union of the two."—Stanley Lane-Poole, " Studies in a Mosque," p. 29.

Mahomet arose to convert them to the purer belief in the One Supreme Deity.

And so back to bed at our primitive inn—"to sleep? to dream?" Alas! no, but to wage warfare with damp sheets, which even in African climes one would rather not have to meet at close quarters. Every one had retired with the exception of a friendly night-porter, whose services my maid enlisted. He did his best to bake them in the oven, but the kitchen fire was out and his efforts were ineffectual; so we ended by passing the night in blankets and discomfort. At least, however, there are no mosquitoes at Blidah. In Algiers these nightly horrors are insatiably ravenous, and the bites they inflict are so much more venomous than those of their European compeers that they positively raise blisters.

We visited next morning the splendid Government stud, where five hundred pure-bred Arab stallions from the Sahara pull at their halters, looking round with wistful eyes at the soldier who calls them by their names. How they would rejoice if they could feel the desert sand shift once more beneath their flying hoofs, instead of being pent up in boxes, or trotting solemnly beneath the accoutrements of the French cavalry! In the spacious barrack-square the soldiers have collected

ARAB BOY AT WELL.

quite a large local menagerie, including some wild monkeys caught in the gorges hard by. There are also a few ostriches ostentatiously paddocked here, for though the French colonizers have been baffled in their attempt to make ostrich-farming succeed in Algeria, they still cling, with all the sentiment of a composer of drawing-room ballads, to the memory of what "might have been."

And now for the glorious Gorges de la Chiffa and the hillside where the monkeys live. As we leave Blidah behind us the scenery grows grander and wilder. Towering rocks, clothed with wild maidenhair, loom on either side of the road, pierced here and there by tunnels, for the Medeah Railway—a triumph of engineering—wends on its unchecked way here, overspanning the Oued el Chiffa on bridges poised in mid-air, or tearing the heart out of the deepest mountains to gain its passage. Waterfalls foam down every rent in the rock and mingle with the torrent below, and but for the smiling blue sky above us the scene would be almost terrifying in its gloomy grandeur. As we alight after a ten kilomètres drive at the Auberge du Ruisseau des Singes, our driver promises us that we shall see monkeys in plenty if we only go far enough; and we set out full of expectancy. The wooded sloping sides of the ravine and the little river below remind one at first sight of Watersmeet in North Devon on a larger scale; but they are like yet unlike, for as one climbs up the steep narrow track the thick trees and plants prove to be all unfamiliar. The English beeches and birches are replaced by cork trees and wild palms, the primroses and bluebells by strange spotted arums and torch irises. On and up we go, as noiselessly as possible, keeping a sharp look-out for the little Simians we have come to visit. We waited and watched long, hoping to see the wistful brown faces peeping forth, and to hear the monkey-folk chatter; but, alas! the afternoon was waxing late and rather chill, and the wee people stayed at home on this occasion; so, as we could not pursue them to the further gorges, we were obliged to return to Blidah after a fruitless errand.

With the expedition to Blidah terminated our visit to Algeria; on leaving which terrestrial paradise one question presents itself, What has France done for the Arabs of this province? For one thing she has delivered them from the bondage of the Turks, who were indeed cruel taskmasters. *En plus*, she has given them regular employment in vineyards, orange-gardens, date-groves, railways, shipping-yards, and a thousand commercial enterprises. She has given them sanitation, police, and civilization in so far as it can be combined with their religious code. She has given them French courts of law where their grievances can be redressed without bribes to corrupt effendis. Their property is secured to them by the *Chefs des bureaux Arabes*, officials who, to their knowledge of European jurisprudence, have added a profound study of the language and customs with which they have to deal, and whose duty it is to inquire into and adjust all disputes between rival tribes, etc.

All this and much more have the French given to the native population; and the native population seem to be duly submissive and grateful, also—at any rate in the time of the Second Empire, if not now—dutifully attached to their new masters. But there is always a reverse to the shield: and there is one open wound here which the yoke never ceases from galling. It must be remembered that their whole social life is based upon their religion, that the slightest violation of the Korán becomes in their eyes a case of absolute sacrilege, a crime against the law of God and His Prophet which may lose them their chance of Paradise, that Mahommedan paradise which is so enchanting that men have been blown from guns without flinching in the hope of reaching it. Moreover, the Musulman conserves, if any one does in these days when universal civilization has obliterated so many landmarks and traditions, all the prejudices of old times. He is no less steeped in fanaticism now than when his forefathers bore the Crescent against the Crusaders. It is hard for us to realize in these days, when Christians of all sects hold their belief quite mildly and with a due regard for the feelings of their brethren, what it must mean to these stern-featured men to watch processions, headed by the emblem of a rival faith, pass unchecked over ground once trodden by the successors of the Prophet. Daily now, too, they have to submit to the careless contempt of the conquering race, daily to see the feet of Roumis defiling their mosques, copies of the sacred Korán exposed to the touch of strangers in the curiosity-shop, cadis and Marabouts alike treated as ordinary citizens, and possibly even—should occasion arise for it—their women's apartments invaded by the French police. The Turks were cruel, but at least they were of the same creed.

To-day, all is outwardly smiling and prosperous; old grudges dead, apparently, and buried deep. But the hatred and treachery of Islam, having lasted for centuries, cannot be exterminated in a few short years, and who can tell what the future keeps for some unguarded moment?* The massacring insurrection of 1871, when the French had their

* See Appendix C.

hands full at home, shows what it is to live over a volcano. And who knows? The great sheikhs, whose word is to the tribes still law, camping out at starlight in the silent desert beyond Biskra, with their flocks and falcons, may sometimes look at the old swords, sometimes think on their grandfathers slain by the battalions of Louis Philippe, and some day perhaps will rise up and say, "Do not Allah and His Prophet bid us revenge the wrongs which His people have suffered?" It may be long in coming, but—*ces choses là ne s'oublient pas!*

TUNISIA.

CHAPTER VII.

ON BOARD THE "ABD-EL-KAD'R."

Our voyage on board the *Abd-el-Kad'r*—Towns on the African coast—An Arab descendant of Saint Louis—Bizerta—A boys' school—A village of outcasts—Arrival at Tunis.

THE cries of the Arabs, who for hours have been busy shipping cargo, have now ceased, the last siren whistle has sounded, and gradually the green slopes of Mustafa, the white tower on the Peñon, and the curves of the Corsairs' Creek fade and grow indistinct, as the great ship *Abd-el-Kad'r*, of the Compagnie Transatlantique, which is to bear us to Tunis, glides on her way.

We numbered only eight first-class passengers (not counting the captain's tame goat, who used to walk about on deck eating salad, and a family of fascinating Persian cats). As everything possible was done to increase our comfort in the way of clean, roomy cabins, a daintily upholstered ladies, drawing-room, and the most *recherché* repasts which the ingenuity of a first-class chef could devise, it seemed more like a trip on a luxurious yacht than a passage on board a coasting vessel. The weather, too, during the whole five days was perfect, with the exception of one night of horror, when the ship and our belongings alike rolled in all directions. I have a vivid recollection of my sufferings on that occasion, and of how the stewardess would totter in after some peculiarly awful crash to pick up the pieces, murmuring in a tone of agony, "*Mon Dieu, quel carnage!*" However, next morning the Mediterranean wore its usual blue and smiling face, and the rest of the voyage passed off peacefully. We had a mighty warrior on board in the shape of an Arab sheikh, who was a veteran soldier in the French army, and displayed many decorations. From constant contact with Europeans he had in some measure rubbed off the edges of his Musulman bigotry, and allowed his young and beautiful wife to come on deck for some hours daily with his little daughter; though of course none of the family could eat at our table. Finding, however, that some Arabs of the lower class could see her from where they sat, the poor lady was promptly muffled up and sent below, where she had to remain for the rest of the voyage, and we beheld her no more. Monsieur le Commandant, who was addicted to chaff, combined with a weakness for discussing British affairs, used to hold forth to us nightly at dinner upon the merits of *le 'Ome Roulle*. Having discovered which way our sympathies lay, he would solemnly asseverate, "Je trouve, moi, que M. Gladstone c'est un brav' homme, tandis que ce blagueur de Marquis," etc.; but like the duchess's baby "when he sneezes" (as her Grace explained to Alice)—

> "He only does it to annoy,
> Because he knows it teases;"

for he possessed to perfection the art of "drawing" one while himself preserving a face of ultra-gravity.

The towns on the Algerian littoral are not interesting from an antiquarian point of view. Most of them have been founded by the French since the conquest; or if one sees here and there the crumbling remains of some bombarded Arab Kasbah, it is only by a rare chance. For the most part they consist of modern quays, a row of fishermen's cottages, and beyond that a grand modern collection of shops, colonnades, and public gardens. At Bône Monsieur le Commissaire dragged us off to see a Roman amphitheatre, with statues and other remains in perfect preservation; but I waved them scornfully aside, and started off mosque-hunting, for is not Europe full of Roman antiquities? and when one is in Africa it is a pity to get one's impressions mixed.

On arriving at Djdjelli a personage of great importance met us, no less a celebrity than the Sidi Bel Kassim Bourbon, a left-handed descendant of the royal line of France! A friend in Algiers, knowing that I was interested in *les indigènes*, had kindly telegraphed to him to meet us, assuring me that he was a great character. Accordingly he stood awaiting us, a tall fine man in a Turkish caftan of black with gold lace, and a fez, and possessing unmistakably the amiable *mouton* features of his regal ancestors, particularly as to the nose and chin. He did the honours of the town, and showed us the mosque, himself rolling aside the carpets, so that we might look in without taking our shoes off, and afterwards took me to visit his own wife and the wives of his brother. The two latter were lovely women, with very fair skins and fine black eyes and hair, but the effect was marred by the fact that they live in a modern house built on the plan of a European cottage, and their Eastern finery looked out of keeping with the bare straight walls of an attic. Mrs. Bel Kassim Bourbon was absent from home (" I let her go out now," he said, " because she is old and ugly!"); but she turned up in time to do the honours of her domain, and insisted on loading me with some splendid home-grown oranges.

On inquiring how he, an Arab of Northern Africa, could be descended from a line of French kings, he explained that in the Middle Ages a handful of French had conquered and held for some years a small settlement on the coast, under the leadership of the Duc de Beaufort, himself an illegitimate son of the then King of France; and, this son of St. Louis added, with a smile and a French shrug of his shoulders, "*Eh bien, madame, c'est arrivé comme cela!*" He is very proud of his lineage, went to Paris for the Exhibition, and always speaks of himself as a Frenchman, not an Arab.

Another cloudless day and calm night, and early next morning we reached Bizerta, and were dressed and ready to land by 6.30 a.m., for the ship only stayed here till ten o'clock, and there is much to see. Bizerta is a perfect specimen of an Arab town, absolutely untouched by European influence. The harbour itself contains some French torpedo boats, and is fringed with a few official buildings; but quickly passing by these, we reach the real old walled city, with its flat white roofs and cupolas. The streets are all level here, and many of them roofed over with curious arches. It is very delightful to wander at will in the cool morning air through a quaint old town like this, peeping through the open shop doors, where, here, some men stand weaving bright-coloured silks at the loom, and there others are carving in wood. The women here wear dark blue veils, completely hiding the face, as they shuffle along to their marketing. We longed to enter the splendid mosques, but our efforts were unsuccessful; for the great fast of Ramadan had begun on the previous day, and the mosque doors were all closed till evening to permit the officials to sleep away as many hours of starvation as possible. A courteous French officer whom we passed told us that the cadi would send a man to open them for us, and directed us to his house; but when we reached it the cadi proved to be fast asleep, like every one else, and so great a personage could not, of course, be disturbed.

We peeped into a boys' school, however, where a turbaned and spectacled old professor was teaching the young idea to shoot. The boys were seated cross-legged round him, merry-looking little gamins, fez on pate, and all their little shoes in a row on the mat outside. I don't expect their studies were very severe; for little reck they of competitive examinations or the School Board fiend, and so long as they can recite the required passages from the Korán, their tutor will probably be quite satisfied.

Beyond the city lies a large salt lake separated from the sea by a tongue of land. We made our way through the market and out again by the city gates, and became aware of a curious village built just outside the walls, the houses even touching them in places; and in the stalls there was no merchandise displayed except a kind of rude pottery. I learned afterwards that it is a village of Andalusian Moors, some of whose ancestors when driven out of Spain came here, as others did to Algiers. But the original Arabs who had conquered Bizerta from the Berbers in 662, and dwelt there ever since, would have nothing to do with them. Then the exiled Moors lifted up their voices and wept, saying, "Are we not true believers and followers of the Prophet even as ye are? and were not our fathers of the same blood as your fathers?" But those within the walls still shut their gates upon them, so that they encamped humbly without. And thus it comes to pass that at Bizerta the ordinary position of affairs is reversed; for whereas in the other cities on the northern coast of Africa it is the Moors who, loving to dwell sumptuously, inhabit the towns, while their Bedawy brethren dwell in mud gourbis on the plains or under tents in the desert, here, on

the contrary, the Arab lives within the shelter of the city walls, while the Moor finds a refuge in the small hamlet that has sprung up outside. They enter Bizerta for marketing purposes, etc., but only marry in their own tribe, which still remains a perfectly distinct one.

Before hailing a boat to take us back to *déjeuner* on the ship we paused before a French café on the quay to take an *apéritif*, which was served by a clean, smiling, white-aproned waiter. What a wonderful animal is your French *garçon de café*! Here he is, exiled with a mere handful of his compatriots in an African town, far from home and friends, and yet at ten a.m. he will don his dress-coat and white *tablier*, and smilingly range his tables and chairs on the pavement, and serve your *vermout de Turin* as briskly as though he were at home in his beloved Paris. Our change was tendered here in the pretty little Tunisian coins, whereby we woke to the fact that we had that morning for the first time entered the dominions of his Highness the Bey of Tunis.

The scenery as one coasts along from Bizerta to Tunis is magnificent—bold cliffs, with mountains in the background, and occasionally a rocky islet upstanding in the blue sea. Nestling in the shadow of the hills lies the town of Suleiman, which appears, as seen from the distance, completely Arab, with its high walls and minarets; a perfect little gem. Possibly one or two French *fonctionnaires* and a few Maltese represent the European element there, but only the white flat-roofed Eastern dwellings are apparent. Along the coast lie large tracts of sand-hills, where seemingly the desert and the sea-shore mingle. Once we passed a solitary koubba, with its white cupolas, on a hillside, doubtless the tomb of some saint who lies there with his face turned towards the sea; for beyond the sea lies the Holy City.

At last the new cathedral of Carthage loomed in sight, and shortly after we beheld Tunis, the "White City," "the Burnous of the Prophet," as it has been poetically styled from its shape. The new canal was not as yet opened, so we had to disembark at La Goulette. It was with many regrets that we bade farewell to M. le Commandant, M. le Commissaire, and all our friends on board, not forgetting the kittens and the goat, and having run the gauntlet of the most disagreeable custom-house officials and the maddest mob of screaming Arab porters I have ever seen, and after a tedious journey in a very slow train through the evil-smelling marshy lake of Behira, we found ourselves in Tunis.

CHAPTER VIII.

TUNIS.

An "arc de triomphe"—In the bazaars—The Dar-ed-Bey—The call to prayer—A caravanserai—The Street of Refuge—A Jewish wedding—A night stroll during Ramadan—The Café Maure.

ONE'S first exclamation is, "*Another* modern town? How very disappointing!" And, indeed, a cursory inspection made between the station and the hotel reveals nothing newer than the usual row of cafés and shops and white streets, where a torchlight *retraite* of the Zouaves in the evening forms the only excitement.

But, halt! What is this great arched doorway which suddenly bursts in majesty upon us? This is the gate of Tunis proper, behind which lies the real town, the Tunis we have come to see, and which, by the splendour of its proportions, makes the fringe of modern buildings that we have just passed look like mere vulgar suburbs. Far from being (as is too often the case with the remaining gates of ancient walled cities) a mere crumbling fragment of masonry bolstered up and huddled in between overtopping modern houses, so hidden that the archæologist has to search toilfully for his treasure, this giant portal forms a dominant feature of the town. So grand and even solemn is it, that one would have thought its own intrinsic merits needed no further recommendation. That there could be any other incentive to its praises never struck me till I came across a sentence in a little French advertising guide to Tunis, published there recently. The Gallic cock must have his crow, and although Tunis is not really added to his poultry-yard, France having, as all the world knows, only a Protectorate there, still, the opportunity is too good to be lost. So he struts up, flaps his wings, and indulges in a prolonged cock-a-doodle-doo. Only hear him! He says, "Terminant l'Avenue de France, une porte monumentale de Tunis antique. Là s'arrêtait jadis la civilization. La France l'ouvrit et y passa le 10 octobre, 1881. Depuis lors, elle est restée debout; mais elle ne ferme plus. Ce n'est donc plus une PORTE. C'est un ARC DE TRIOMPHE: celui du progrès sur la Barbarie! On l'a baptisée: *Porte de France!*" How truly French!

Without stopping to consider whether we shall

regard it in the light of a French triumphal arch or not, let us pass through it, and, as the fairy tales of our childhood used to say, " You shall see what you shall see."

First, a busy hum of voices attracts us, and, pressing forward, we find ourselves near the entrance to the *souks*, or bazaars—long, obscure, tunnel-like streets, whose arched roofs, save for here and there a skylight, shut out the glaring sun. An entire street is devoted to the manufacture and sale of a particular article. Thus we see the Souk-el-Attarin, or Bazaar of the Perfumers; the Souk-el-Seradjin, or Bazaar of the Saddlers, etc. The different "shops" in each souk are no more than dens, in the doorways of which the vendors sit, with their completed wares piled up beside them, and their hands busily turning out more to swell the number. The principal goods on sale are saddlery, arms, shoes, stuffs, embroideries, *checchias* or fez-caps, perfumes, henna, books, sweetmeats, etc. The Tunisian saddlery is superlatively gorgeous. On a foundation of red and green velvet, brass ornaments and studs are thickly constellated in every conceivable device; and the heavy trappings are well calculated to show off the dark sleek skins of the mules, which are here esteemed more highly than horses. The Street of the Shoemakers is full of men's bright yellow morocco-leather slippers turned "down-at-heel," varied here and there by small ones in blushing rose-colour, white, or delicate green, affected by the fair sex; to these latter, gold embroidery is generally added. In a more sombre section the checchia cap finds its birthplace. The red felt is cut out, and moulded into the proper shape on wooden blocks. Next to the fez-makers come the sellers of henna, with sacks piled full of the leaves of this plant on one side of their open doors, and dishes full of the same leaves ready powdered for use at the other. An infusion of the powder in warm water will tint the finger-tips with the rich red-brown tint, which lasts for weeks, and which the Arabs consider such an enhancement of beauty; but the powder must be kept from touching stuffs or linen, on which it will leave an ineradicable stain.

Round a corner we came suddenly upon the vendors of *bric-à-brac*, on whose stalls lie, in gorgeous confusion, embroideries from Stamboul, swords from Damascus, tables incrusted in one iridescent sheath of mother-of-pearl, carpets, brass trays, and every conceivable bibelot. One of the merchants, Ahmed Djamal by name, who had a really splendid collection, and whose shop boasted of a second story, pressed us to enter, and politely regretted that he could not offer us coffee, as during Ramadan no strict Musulman may allow a morsel of food or drop of drink to cross his threshold between dawn and sunset.

But how paint the glories of jewellery, coloured burnouses, gold-embroidered *portières*, women's brocaded vestures, *sendouks* (*i.e.* bride-chests), brackets and couches brilliant with gold and colour, and the thousand other beautiful objects near which one longs to linger? To take it all in comfortably is an impossible feat, for the narrow bazaars are crowded almost to suffocation with a shouting, jostling crowd, and it is all one can do to keep one's feet in places. Sellers rush out from their dens crying some just-completed article which they hold up aloft. Buyers shout out conflicting bids for that same, and, anon, all have to make way for an incoming string of asses, which file down the central gutter, bearing fresh supplies to this busy mart. The animation and noise here form a curious contrast to the silent and almost empty streets of Old Algiers. People who have seen both often make comparisons between them disparaging to the latter; but, for my part, I think that each possesses its own separate style of beauty, as incomparable as sunlight with moonlight. Though Tunis, being less Europeanized, retains more purity of local colour, yet the languid, dream-like stillness of Algiers will always have a soothing charm for me.

In the very heart of the souks, where four ways meet in a large central square, is the "Souk-el-Birka," where once, as its name denotes, the ancient slave-market was held, and where human wares were bought and sold busily before the abolition of this horrible trade. The principal mosque, "Es-Zitouna," supported on a magnificent row of pillars brought from Carthage, runs parallel with the Street of the Perfumers, so that it is easy for the Tunisian merchants to pass from business to devotion when the call to prayer is heard. And what is this oblong barrier rising out of the pavement that cleaves the throng of buyers and sellers in twain? It is a wooden coffin of the sacred green colour, having at one corner an iron socket to hold the candle which is lighted here, as at every sacred shrine, on Fridays and feast-days. For in the earth, below this symbolical coffin, lie the remains of one of the greatest Marabouts of Tunisian history, and the fact that his grave is there is believed to protect this street, and to bring good luck to the merchants in it.

Leaving the souks we emerge into the more open streets of the town. And here one is continually

TUNISIAN SOUKS.

struck by finding a doorway upheld on marble pillars, or a bit of carved stone let into a wall, which the eye at once distinguishes as pre-eminently *un-*Moorish. "The reason is not far to find;" they are merely bits of poor, old, ruined Carthage, which for countless ages has been pillaged to adorn the buildings of younger cities. Slight local peculiarities are noticeable here; for these African towns, though having a surface similarity, differ greatly in detail from each other. For instance, the house-doors, which at Algiers were low, and either of perfectly plain wood or else divided into irregular panels, and which at Bizerta were coloured brilliant red or green, have here blossomed into tall and graceful portals, covered thickly with iron studding arranged in the most flowing arabesques. In these such designs as the hand of Fatma, the Seal of Solomon, the Crescent, etc., are blended harmoniously. Again, we have seen that the women of Algiers are trousered, and wear white face-veils, leaving the eyes and part of the forehead exposed to view; while at Blidah only a corner of one eye was visible. Here in Tunis an extraordinary transformation has come over the scene, for white veils and baggy pantaloons have alike disappeared, and in their place are tight leggings, which encase them from the ankle to the thigh in mummy-like wrappings, and the face is covered entirely in *black* crape, with only the thinnest possible slit of the eyes to see through. Issuing, as it does, from the white *haick*, this sable veil has a most lugubrious and startling effect, suggestive of the black-masked executioners of the Middle Ages; and the tight leg-swathings, besides being hideously inartistic, do not fulfil the conventional idea of a Moslem woman's attire half as well as the balloony trousers.

The Dar-ed-Bey, or town palace of the sovereign, stands just beyond the souks, looking down with paternal interest, *en bon roi*, on its busy subjects. In internal decoration it is indeed a gem, the friezes and ceilings being particularly rich in the lacy, raised stucco-work for which Arabian architecture is famous. Arches of black and white marble surround the great central patio leading to the throneroom, where the Bey occasionally receives the foreign ambassadors in state. Upstairs we were shown a room commanding the busiest streets, with a balcony on which his Highness can show himself in full view of his people; but he rarely stays here now, preferring his country palace at Marsa. Our guide then hurried us up a small side staircase on to the flat roof of the palace in time to be at the midday call to prayer. On the minaret of every mosque may be observed its attendants with eyes anxiously fixed on the tower of the principal one, El Djemâa-es-Zitouna, whose tall tower dominates all the rest. Punctually at the Moslem noon (about three-quarters of an hour in advance of our time) the two mueddins appear on the little balcony running round it, and hoist the white flag, which is to give the signal to the whole city. And in one moment the air is filled with voices, as from every one of their giddy perches these men proclaim the "Allah-il-Allah," and the faithful betake themselves to prayer. Alas! these roofs and minarets are all we are ever destined to see of the beautiful mosques of Tunis, for being still an unconquered nation, the Tunisians will not suffer the Roumis to enter them, as their down-trodden Algerian brethren are forced to do. With strange inconsistency, however, they allow strangers to visit those of Kerouan, the sacred city; but probably this is because fewer travellers penetrate there. Three of the largest mosques in Tunis are dedicated respectively to Sidi Yussuf, Sidi Ben-Aroussa, and Sidi Mahrez; and amongst the patron saints of the town are Lalla Manoulia, a woman who, having in her lifetime made and kept a vow of chastity, is said to have received after death the power of working miracles, and Sidi Fath-Allah, a Marabout, to whose grave, on a hill east of the city, women desirous of having children must climb, repeating the first verses of the Korán till they reach the summit, where they invoke the prayers of the saint.

Further on lies the Jewish quarter; then a semi-European part, inhabited by the numerous Maltese who crowd Tunis; and then again an outlying Arab quarter reaching the outskirts of the town. Here you may see strings of camels peacocking along the narrow alleys, bringing merchandise from far inland. Here, too, are the *fondouks*, or caravanserai, where rest for man and beast may be had. They look gloomy and inhospitable enough to our ideas, but to theirs probably furnish all that is requisite. Little cell-like sheds open off a large central square all the way round, unfurnished and uncarpeted. In one of these aching voids a traveller will spread his own mat, which, like his food, he must carry with him; and his camel kneels, tethered, in front of it. Thus they repose till morning, when the reckoning is paid, and man and beast go on their way together.

Among the localities worthy of note in this quarter is the Street of Refuge, where evil-doers can take sanctuary; and once there they are safe from justice. This street is consecrated to the memory of the great Sheikh and Marabout, Sidi Mahrez, whose tomb is hard by. And they of Tunis tell a tale of how he caused a khelouat (or small zaouia) to be miraculously constructed in one night by the king of the Jinns, with a rampart and a gateway, which was thenceforth called Bab el Djedid (the New Gate). He was a holy man, and renowned in the working of miracles; and may Allah grant us participation in the favours vouchsafed to him, and place us with him in the Day of the Resurrection. Amin!

Now and again you may see a water-carrier bearing on his back a wild-boar's skin, full to bursting of the precious fluid, and the bristles, wetted by escaping drops, glisten in the sunshine. A sorcerer sits in his narrow den who would be delighted to show one a little serpent-charming, only it is Ramadan time (an excuse which is very useful when they want to get out of doing anything), but who will tattoo you artistically—should you desire it—for a trifling consideration. But we must now retrace our steps to the Jewish quarter, for we have been invited to witness a Hebrew wedding, which, from the peculiar gorgeousness of the Tunisian Jewesses' costumes, is a most important sight; and it is time to start for the synagogue.

This edifice is poor, dirty, and badly lighted; very different from the one at Algiers, which rivalled the mosques in its magnificence. After we have sat in semi-darkness for some time, there is a stir at the door, and some twenty little boys walk in two by two, chanting psalms, followed by the bridegroom, a tall, fair young man in a dark kaftan, having round his shoulders a black-and-white striped scarf, which is destined to play an important part in the ceremonial. He was accompanied by a number of men, who sat with a bored expression on their faces while the rabbi intoned more psalms and prayers. This over, they all filed out, we following the procession, *en route* for the bride's house, where the concluding and most interesting ceremonies were to take place. (N.B.—The women do not go to the synagogue.) We take up our position in the courtyard, against one wall of which a high platform has been constructed, on which is placed a chair. The bridegroom, still wearing on his shoulders that extraordinary shawl, which reminds one of a chilly old lady, is accommodated with another chair on the ground in line with the platform, the rabbis standing in front.

After a long wait, down comes the bride from her chamber, accompanied by her mother (her father is dead). Both ladies are indeed "a sight for to see," and I now begin to realize why no visit to Tunis is considered complete without a sight of a Tunisian Jewess's wedding. Our bride on this occasion was attired in a loose chemise-like tunic, descending nearly to the knees, of the most exquisite pale-blue brocaded satin, just open enough at the throat to disclose the collar of an undervest stiff with gold embroidery, and having secondary sleeves of floating gauze. Her legs were tightly encased in the regulation *culottes collantes*, which seemed literally like sheaths of gold, so thickly encrusted were they with stripes of gold lace, masses of raised gold embroidery, and clusters of golden spangles. On the back of her head perched the little conical cap, in shape like a coronet, supposed to be the descendant of the Phrygian cap, and from its point a white wimple floated down her back. She scintillated with diamond rings and brooches, as did her mother, whose outer tunic of mauve satin, golden cap, and leggings were in no way less gorgeous than her daughter's. Both ladies had attained to the height of *embonpoint* necessary for Tunisian beauties, who when young undergo special dieting in order to arrive at the proper pitch of fatness. To our eyes it naturally seems hideous, but in Tunis, when a woman can scarcely drag her unwieldy bulk along with slow, unsteady footsteps, while her flesh seems to close over the rings and bracelets she wears, she is considered to be at the zenith of her charms.

No sign of recognition was exchanged between

bride and bridegroom, who might both have been jointed wooden dolls. This is part of the proper etiquette at these weddings, where the bride is expected to behave as though she were an automaton. Her mother, having helped her to mount on to the platform, arranged the girl's dress, disposed her hands, etc., much as a photographer does when placing his victim in position, she herself not making a single spontaneous movement, but looking down on the spectators from her high throne with an impassive countenance. The chief rabbi having intoned more psalms and prayers out of a Hebrew book, the *raison d'être* of the black-and-white scarf next became apparent, for the end nearest to the bride was raised by an assistant and passed over her tall cap, thus sheltering both under the same canopy. The ring was then placed on the bride's finger, while at the same moment a perfect yell of " You-you-you-you-you-ee's " rose from the friends in the gallery above. Then a nasty muddy-looking fluid (query, wine?) was brought in, ceremonially mixed with water, and handed round amongst the parties concerned till each had taken a sip, and the glass was then shivered to atoms on the ground to more shouts of "You-you-ee," bringing the ceremony to a close. The whole *cortège* then proceeded upstairs, we following. Arrived there, the splendour was perfectly dazzling, for full a hundred guests were present, all attired in the same fashion, and with equally lavish use of gold on pointed caps and culottes. One might be behind the scenes of Drury Lane at a dress rehearsal; only instead of cotton velvet and tinsel shams, the brocades were stiff enough to stand alone, and the garish laces and spangles were of pure gold. They must have represented a fabulous sum; and the furniture of the house was in keeping with the dresses, showing that the children of Israel have not yet lost the secret of spoiling the Egyptians. The bride being seated in the post of honour, the women friends advanced one by one to kiss her; and a lock of her hair, together with a fragment of her veil, were cut off by her mother; after which, amid preparations for the feast which ends the day's proceedings, we retired. At midnight she must set out for her husband's house, with the proper ceremonies suggestive of her reluctance; such as taking three steps forward and two backwards, so that her transit occupies some time. Her friends then leave her in the connubial nest, and the following day she holds another great reception in her new home. I am glad to have seen such a gathering of the *haute Juiverie*; who, in spite of kohled eyelids, henna-tinted fingers, and preponderant fat, were handsome women, possessed of ivory skins, beautiful dark eyes, and oval faces.

As we retrace our steps through the Jewish quarter, we pass numerous poorer members of the community in common leggings of stuff minus the gold lace, and whose conical caps are covered by a black silk handkerchief, either to protect the embroidery on working days, or else because they cannot boast of that embellishment. The men wear the same costume as the Moors, only in darker colours, and either the plain fez or a dark blue turban. As we passed one open house-door we paused in the gateway to watch them kneading the unleavened bread for the approaching Passover.

A visit to Tunis during the month of Ramadan would be incomplete without an inspection of the Arab town by night. Accordingly after dinner we tramp off to it again in the company of our native guide. This fast begins annually from the very moment when two reliable watchmen announce the appearance of the new moon which ushers in the sacred month. For three days before the fast begins no wine may be drunk, and throughout its duration eating, drinking, and smoking are forbidden from dawn to sunset. When the latter blissful moment arrives, therefore, it will readily be believed that the faithful—who have been

THE CITY OF TUNIS.

exhaustedly "lying low" all day and sleeping as long as possible to abate the pangs of hunger—lose no time in breaking their fast. They begin by swallowing three mouthfuls of water, with dates or other trifles, in pronouncing the formula: "Ia Allah! I have fasted in obedience to Thy will; and I break my fast now by eating of Thy bounties." From this moment they feast abundantly, till their suspended animation breaks out afresh with their returning strength; and the wildest revelry and often license prevails in the streets and houses. Far from being, like our Lent, a time of penitence, the nights of Ramadan are more suggestive of feasting than fasting. Conjurers and *danseuses* perform in temporary booths to crowded houses; even a strolling French fair, with shooting-galleries and merry-go-rounds, finds favour with the swarthy merry-makers. The minarets of every mosque are brilliantly illuminated with lamps which outline their graceful proportions. In one corner the smokers are tasting the dreamy joys conveyed by haschish pipes; in another, public scribes and notaries are busy at the dictation of their unlettered clients. Buyers and sellers of every kind of food haggle at the tops of their voices; the beat of tomtoms indicates the direction of various side-shows, which our guide hints that it would not be edifying for us to witness; and through the crowd quietly circulate the ubiquitous French police, on the alert to stop the brawls to which the excited condition of the populace on these occasions often leads, and which sometimes terminate in bloodshed.

A glance in at a Café Maure terminates the evening. Though larger and more important looking than any I had seen at Algiers or Blidah, the performance was not so good. To the strains of the musicians seated in a row behind them, several Almées went through the usual posturings, but in a very sleepy and uninterested manner. Perhaps the Ramadan fast had robbed them of their strength, for the only one who put the slightest animation into her work was a young and very pretty Jewess. But the performance seemed to amply satisfy a youthful Bedawi Arab from the country, who, with a sprig of jasmine stuck in his turban, gazed enraptured and open-eyed at the scene. How much alike human nature is all the world over, and how it reminded us of the "Algies" and "Berties" who, to vary the diversions of hunting or shooting, "come up" for a week's dissipation, and gaze from their stalls at the Frivolity on the *pas de deux* of the Sisters Mash'em.

CHAPTER IX.

TUNIS.

The Bardo—A secret door—The Hall of Justice—An unlucky prophet—Palace of Kassar-Saïd—A state bed—The ruins of Carthage—A subterranean dwelling—The royal mausoleum—A perfumer's shop—A rich house in Tunis—The cadi's "divan"—*La mort sans phrase*—Envoi.

WHEN a Bey of Tunis dies, that one of his palaces which has witnessed his demise is at once deserted by his successor and left to desolation; from which causes Tunis and its environs are full of such abandoned buildings more or less gone to decay. The most beautiful of all these royal residences is unquestionably the Bardo, and though not inhabited by the present Bey for the reason given above, it is still the official seat to which he repairs on certain occasions, as for signing treaties, delivering sentence of death, or conducting other business of state. Some of his officials have permanent quarters there.

The walled village and fortress, with this great

palace in its midst, which form together the mass of buildings known as the Bardo, is about two kilomètres from Tunis. On approaching the gates of the little town you might imagine yourself in some mediæval citadel of Europe. After passing through several streets, mostly inhabited by poor people, with here and there the larger house of some Court official, the Government offices, soldiers' barracks, etc., we arrive at the palace itself. A great portion of it is now ruinous, and is being demolished in the interests of the public safety. This is no doubt necessary and wise; but one cannot help looking regretfully at the heaps of *débris*, among which beautiful old tiles and fragments of stucco-ornament lift their heads. We gain the central court by the celebrated staircase of the Lions. Eight of these marble beasts guard the stair, four on either side; every lion in a different attitude, and all equally life-like. They were brought from Italy, and the stamp of the civilized art to which they owe their creation, visible in their every line, forms a curious contrast to the barbaric Eastern splendour of the patio which lies beyond them.

Out of this court lead several magnificent rooms, notably that called the Salle des Psychés, from the enormous sheets of glass with which the walls and ceiling are lined. Upstairs is the Salle de

Café (now turned into a museum of local Roman remains), which rejoices in an immense domed roof richly gilded. In this room the Bey of old was wont to sit and drink his coffee surrounded by the entire Court. By special favour I was allowed to pass through a secret door at one end of it, to which the public in general are not admitted. This door, screened by an embroidered *portière*, is made to turn noiselessly on a pivot by means of a concealed spring, and opens into a labyrinth of narrow, pitch-dark passages, each leading to a different room. For the secret door is the barrier between the palace and the sacred precincts of the royal harem, in which, besides the separate apartments of the four legitimate Beyesses, quarters were found for numerous odalisques as well; and by this private entrance the Bey could steal alone and unperceived into the bower of whichever fair lady it might be his royal pleasure to visit. A glass door at the end of one of these small passages gives access to the terrace and harem garden.

The Mahkamma, or Hall of Justice, is perhaps the most splendid thing in the whole palace, where splendour abounds. Of oblong shape, its walls are lined with ancient marbles, the spoil of Carthage, displayed in panels of giallo-antico, rosso-antico, and lapis lazuli. A double row of pillars gives a church-

M

like effect to the room, and between the arches are placed low satin divans. At the further end stands the great throne on which the Bey sits to administer justice to his subjects. This throne is flanked on either side by two short black marble columns from Carthage, which have a particularly solemn effect in the midst of so much glitter; in the back of the chair is embedded a diamond ornament, the gift of the Sultan of Turkey; above it shines the crescent with a star between its horns on an achievement of banners, and a canopy of state overtops the whole. Verses from the Korán are inscribed on the frieze. To this supreme tribunal prisoners found guilty in the inferior court of the cadi, are brought to receive their final sentence from the Bey himself. The reigning Bey, now that he no longer resides here, arrives from his palace at Marsa by special train for this purpose. He fasts for a whole day before signing the death-warrant, and on taking his seat on the throne smokes his pipe in silence. The passing of his hand across his moustache is the signal of doom, and the prisoner is led out by the guards and executed on a little square, which we were shown, immediately outside the palace. The terrible bastinado which used to precede death has been abolished since the French occupation of Tunisia. There still exists a curious custom of ransoming criminals, called the *achat du sang*, by which, if the friends of the condemned man are able to pay into the beylical treasury the required sum within a certain time after sentence has been pronounced in the cadi's court, his life is purchased and he is free once more.

The Salle de Réception is more European in its decoration, and is chiefly remarkable for the full-length portraits of sovereigns presented to various Beys. Here are Louis Philippe, Victor Emmanuel, Napoleon III. (by Winterhalter), and others; together with the fine portrait of Mustafa, the last Bey who ever wore the complete Moorish dress. He looks the very impersonation of a warlike "Grand Turk," with his kaftan of the royal green, and his flowing grey beard. His turban and the hilt of his scimetar are blazing with jewels. Ahmed Bey, who succeeded him in 1837, adopted the sad garb of a European gentleman (of course excepting the fez, which no Moslem may ever discard), and the three who have filled the throne since then—Mahommed, Mahommed-es-Sadok, and the actual sovereign, Ali Bey—have all been much too grand and civilized to return to the more beautiful costume of their nation. From the Salle de Réception opens the Great Hall of the Pachas, another throne-room, where the Bey receives two or three times a year the blessing of the grand

Marabout. It must be very impressive to see this holy man with outstretched hands—his assistants at either side of him—pronouncing the benediction over the Bey, who sits on the throne, bending his head forwards to receive it. Unfortunately his Highness is now a very old and infirm man, to whom even the short train journey from Marsa is a great effort; so that these ceremonies at the Bardo have of late years been much curtailed, and even dispensed with when possible. A curious prophecy is said to have been delivered by one of these Marabouts in this very room.

It was two years before Mahommed-es-Sadok Bey signed the treaty with France, of which at that time he had not the slightest idea. To him entered, in the Hall of the Pachas, the Marabout wearing, in lieu of a turban, the head-dress of the infidel dogs (*Anglicé*, a European hat, though whether chimney-pot or wideawake history does not relate). It being the most fearful crime for a Musulman to put off the time-honoured *checchia*, the Bey sternly asked the saint why he had ventured into the presence thus attired. The Marabout replied, "Sire, I do it in order that you may know that within two years from this day, your capital will be in the occupation of the French, who will come into it wearing hats like this." The Bey, incensed at hearing this (to him) impossible nonsense, wished to put the Marabout to death; but as the good man came of a very great family, who had for generations been Marabouts, and as his execution, therefore, might have roused the populace to anger, his courtiers persuaded the Bey that the Marabout must have gone suddenly mad, and at last succeeded in getting his sentence reduced to banishment to Kerouan. When, two years later, his prophecy came true, all hastened to the place of his exile to do him honour as a prophet; and he still dwells at Kerouan, an aged and highly venerated man.

As we leave the Bardo, I notice a little cupola denoting the presence of a Marabout's tomb embedded in the outer wall of the palace, and learn that a saint was buried actually in the wall, in order that his body might protect the building should the enemy ever beset it. These Marabouts are very useful, certainly; and when they depart this life their remains seem to be quite as effective as their living selves were.

At a short distance from the Bardo stands another royal palace, that of Kassar-Saïd, anciently the residence of the Bey's chief legitimate wife, though various Beys have made it their own abode from time to time. At present it is quite deserted. More European in its furnishing, it falls far below the Bardo in interest. Indeed, two of the state rooms are chiefly remarkable for the number of French clocks they contain! As many gilt timepieces as would be thought sufficient with us for the drawing-rooms of an entire street are here crowded into these two apartments, and, combined with threadbare Brussels carpets of glaring pattern, and suites of walnut wood and red rep, dating from the early Victorian period, made up an *ensemble* of as glaring bad taste as one could possibly wish *not* to see. But the state bedroom of the Beyess—to whose quondam occupier all this gaudy lodginghouse furniture no doubt represented the highest exotic *luxe*—the state bedroom, I repeat, makes ample amends for all these horrors. On this threshold, at any rate, the foot of the upholsterer from over-seas has paused, and the taste of Araby the Blest has been allowed full play. What a glorious yet exquisite whole is the result!—the doors and ceiling, on which flowery Persian decorations relieve the ancient mellow gold grounds; the rich rugs; the richer brocades and fringed cloths of gold and silver, which drape every doorway; the great semi-circular recess, where her slaves were wont to disrobe their mistress; the painted chests, where once her jewels and her broidered dresses reposed; the soft couches and the silken cushions; and, above all, the twin

BEY'S BED, PALACE OF KASSAR-SAÏD.

beds of the Bey and Beyess, each in their tiled alcove, which exemplify what an Arabian bedstead really *is*. In a poor or a middle-class interior it means a high structure, covered with a shapeless conglomeration of rugs, placed against one wall, and screened off from the rest of the room with a curtain. In the homes of the mighty it means the crowning glory, the dazzling triumph of furniture which the accompanying illustration will describe better than could my humble pen. Suffice it to say, that the entire sides, the head and foot, and the low canopy, with its dependent frieze, are formed completely of crystal, over which meander waves of raised golden tracery; and in this glittering nest, which a fairy with a wave of her wand might have consolidated for some story-princess, the royal slumberer reposes between sheets of silk and satin coverlets. No wonder the " Tales of the Thousand and One Nights " were invented in bed, with *such* a bed to promote soft imaginings. What couches like these must have cost one shudders to think of; and what would the result be if some clumsy housemaid (or do they not indulge in such luxuries?) were to shiver that sheeny glass edging to atoms with her broom-handle? But let us draw a veil over such a harrowing possibility. The bath-rooms of the Bey and Beyess open off opposite sides of this state apartment; and beyond them are a series of smaller rooms for the suite; also the Cabinet d'Affaires, where Mahommed-es-Sadok Bey signed the convention with the French. In accordance with the original purpose for which the palace was built, every window is closely veiled with lattice-work, so that without fear of being seen its fair owner might look out on the great orange grove below, whose fragrance, bolder than a lover's glance, could penetrate where he dared not, and rest on her caressingly. We took a turn in this celebrated grove, just then in full blossom; and along an avenue bordered by stone eagles on pedestals, the gift—together with some fine examples of Empire furniture, which we had noted inside the palace—of Napoleon the First to a former Bey; and so out through the great gates guarded by a sentry, whose duties were not too arduous to prevent his stepping forward to present me with a bunch of roses.

Driving back in the cool evening to Tunis along a road dominated by a curious old *bordj*, or fortress, we encountered, first, a string of mules caparisoned with all the elaboration of red velvet and spangles which we had previously so much admired in the bazaars; and secondly, an Arab sportsman with his dog and gun going in quest of the succulent quail. From this point, too, we had a splendid view of the

Zaghouan Mountains and the great salt lake El Bahira, in whose creeks, I was assured, flamingoes might be seen in plenty; but, alas! like the monkeys at the Ruisseau des Singes, they came not to my wishful gaze.

It had long been a dream of mine to sit, like Marius of old, amongst the ruins of Carthage. But when, after a brief railway journey, we arrived on the scene, my ardour was somewhat damped by the fact that there are no longer any ruins to sit amongst! Nothing but a bare expanse of grass, winding gently uphill, and crowned by a brand-new red-brick cathedral—such is Carthage to-day. Alas! if you would see Carthage, you must seek her in the walls of later Tunis, in the cathedral of Pisa, in the churches of Genoa, in the palaces of princes, in the museums of savants—anywhere and everywhere but in the place that knows her no more. Yes, gone are the altars where Hannibal sacrificed; gone is the throne of the great Queen of the old world; gone are the wharves and markets of the Phœnician merchants; and the stones of her strong places and the marbles of her temples have been pillaged to buttress the walls and enhance the beauties of younger cities. "*Carthage, dispersée dans le monde entier, est partout et n'est nulle part.*" *

* Leon Michel, "Tunis," p. 52.

Two things alone remain—the cisterns and the graves. The necropolis, containing the latter, lies across the road at some distance below the site of the town, and every grave has its arrangements for cremation still complete.

The former consist of a long chain of subterraneous aqueducts, and in these underground places a tribe of Bedawys have made their abode, and having walled round the area and fashioned a mosque, they live there contentedly. Thus it comes to pass that the conduits which once brought water to lave the feet of Dido now shelter the only living things besides scorpions that break the eternal rest of Carthage. We descended into the deepest and darkest of these long tunnels, which seemed to pursue its way endlessly below the surface of the earth. Broken up into living rooms and a cowshed, it formed the house of a poor old woman, her children, and her live stock. She welcomed us prettily, clad in the dark blue garb of the Tunisian Bedawys, and unveiled after their fashion; and her poor wrinkled face lighted up when I spoke to her in Arabic. I pitied her profoundly when she told me that she was a widow, and lived here all alone with her children. Lifting her hand to heaven, she said, " I have no one here to take care of me now; only Allah remains." Her simple faith so touched me that, seizing her hand, I said, "*El hamdou lillah, ia mesqina, Allah inoub*" ("Praise be to Allah, oh poor one, He will provide for thee"), and a few silver pieces poured into her palm left her thoroughly cheerful, with the additional advantage—if Sidi Es-Siyouthi speaks truth—of entitling the donors to some extra inches of green robe in the next world.

The Chapel of Saint Louis, on the site of the temple of Esculapius, is in the wretched pseudo-Gothic taste of Louis Philippe's days, and now that the Rois de France and the Roi des Français have alike become things of the past, and a Republic rules which cares for neither, the poor little edifice has a neglected and weather-worn appearance. Indeed, the saint's memory in this locality receives nowadays more veneration from Moors than Christians; for they have started a theory that with his dying breath he embraced Mahommedanism, and is now a Moslem saint, and they accordingly revere the royal Crusader under the name of Sidi Bou-Saïd. As for the new cathedral and monastery of the Pères Blancs, they are very large, very red, and singularly out of keeping with their surroundings. The museum attached to the monastery contains an interesting collection—the result of the excavations made by the White Fathers—of Punic, Phœnician, and Roman remains, with a few relics of early Christian times. We were presented to Père Delattre, the learned prior, whose special pride and delight these *fouilles* are. He seemed to feel the recent loss of Cardinal Lavigerie greatly, and told me he was beside him when he died.

To the train by which we were to return to Tunis was attached a royal saloon carriage, and from it alighted the heir apparent, brother of the Bey. (In Tunisia, the Bey is invariably succeeded by his next surviving brother, or the latter's heirs, to the exclusion of his own sons.) The prince, who was going to his country house near Marsa, seemed old and feeble, and leaned heavily on the arm of one of his suite, while the Arabs round pressed up to kiss his hand. The same royal family—that of Hussein—have reigned since 1691. Once, strolling through the lanes and *impasses* in the heart of Tunis, we came upon an imposing koubba, round which a group of people were collected, and which was no less than the royal mausoleum where all the Beys are buried. Usually kept jealously shut up, on this occasion the guardian had carelessly left open a little crack of one window-shutter; and we flattened our noses in company with the other peering spectators in the hope of seeing something of the glories within. The interior was very grand

and solemn, with its straight lines of simple tombstones of the usual Arabic shape, and here and there a bier covered with rich hangings. Why it should have been built on this spot, far from any of the royal palaces, and, as it were, *à propos* of nothing in particular, I cannot conjecture. Probably it dates from a time when the land was less thickly built over, and the houses which have now sprung up round it did not exist. The remains of the common herd lie in the large cemetery outside the Bab-el-Zouika; but the same fanaticism which forbids strangers to enter the mosques here applies equally to the burying-ground.

I was very anxious to be allowed to see the Bey's harem, and to have an audience of the royal ladies; but this is no longer an easy matter. Formerly the British Consul was able to obtain the favour for ladies of his nation, but since the French occupation this privilege has been withdrawn from the various consulates. On the day before our departure we made the acquaintance of General V——, the Bey's aide-de-camp, who is all-powerful at Court, and who assured me that he would have great pleasure in arranging the affair for me. As he added, however, that it would demand four or five days of correspondence with various other Court officials, I was reluctantly obliged to renounce the project for want of time. His Excellency is a fine-looking man, in European costume with the exception of the fez; he wore a splendid ruby and diamond pin, and a frock coat, on the cuffs of which silver stars were embroidered, to denote his military rank. He has been chosen for the high post he occupies about the Bey for his extreme courtesy and tact, and for his perfect French. Being of Jewish extraction, too, he does not suffer from the *gêne* of a Moslem's religious prejudices in his intercourse with Europeans.

To make up for this disappointment, however, H.B.M. Vice-Consul was kind enough to procure me permission to visit another rich interior, and sent his own janissary to take me to them. This magnificent being, on whose fez was a silver brooch with "V.R.," could not speak a word of anything but Arabic. He is a relic of the retinues of native guards attached to all the consulates in the good old savage times. Nowadays, though they still keep the name of "janissaries," with its fierce associations, they have degenerated into a sort of dragoman—a "harmless, necessary" hanger-on and messenger.

My pseudo-warrior and I proceeded through the bazaars at a swinging pace, only pausing once in the Souk-el-Attarin to be introduced to a friend of his, who was a seller of perfumes by trade, and who allowed me to inhale the contents of all his mysterious little jars. He was much gratified on finding that I could speak Arabic, but declined to believe that I could write it; till I took out my pencil, and traced a compliment or two, such as— ‎دارك‎ ‎زين،‎ ("Thy house is pretty"). Full of laughing delight at the idea of an English lady having mastered his native hieroglyphics, he insisted on presenting me with a pomander box as a souvenir. Taking a little carved rosewood receptacle from the shelf, he proceeded to fill it accordingly with musk-scented lard out of one jar, then added some oil of ambergris from another, laying on top of all a little twist of cotton wool which he had first steeped in a few drops of the precious attar of roses. The little round lid was screwed down on this judicious mingling, and now I know the secret of that baffling mixture of perfumes which exudes from these little appendages so often worn round the necks of Eastern women. He refused all payment, and after some more compliments we proceeded to our destination.

A rich private house in Tunis is a very magnificent affair indeed, vying closely with the Bey's palaces in all but size. At the door I was handed over to a small boy, the son of the house, still young enough to have access to the women's rooms, which in this instance were on the ground floor. As other engagements obliged me to time my visit in the forenoon, house and ladies were alike *en papillotes;* but the hostesses were most pleasant and hospitable, and seemed delighted to trot out all their smart things for my contemplation. One fact I begin to grasp firmly, and that is, that the richer a Moor is the more ormolu clocks, looking-glasses, and wax flowers under shades will he possess himself of; and furniture which with us would nowadays be consigned to the housekeeper's room, is by him imported at great expense to become the pride and joy of the entire family. Whenever, in a Moorish house, I have fallen into raptures over some exquisite native table, or *étagère,* which has as yet escaped banishment, and mention that for years I have had in my English home a boudoir entirely fitted up in Moorish style, I am met with looks of polite amazement. However, in this house much of the homegrown *luxe* had been allowed to survive, and I saw two more of those magnificent Arabian bedsteads of glass and gilt wood, quite as grand as the ones at Kassar-Saïd; from which, and the rest of the finery shown me, I gathered that my entertainers were very great swells indeed. Opening a cabinet whose doors were literally plastered with mother-of-pearl, the ladies produced their best frocks. Oh, what glittering acres of gold-spangled embroidery, filmy gauzes, and silver brocades! When their toilettes were completed, Solomon in all his glory could scarcely have vied with them. A Korán reposed in a casket of solid silver, a *sendouk* which held their robes was thickly covered with gold and silver leaf, and with strange devices in deftly blended hues. Through room after room they led me, showing me the household loom, to which some strands of grass-green silk clung ready for weaving ; and the Jewish women-servants busy at their work. (In many Tunisian houses it is the custom to employ Jewesses, on account of their being able to go out unveiled and with greater freedom on domestic errands.) So many treasures did I see, that by the time I took my leave I was completely dazzled, and felt as Aladdin must have done when he first entered the cave. Poor things! I dare say they get tired of playing with their gold and silver toys, as children do of their wooden ones; and certainly the bright-plumaged bird hanging up in the courtyard in his fantastically painted cage, is not a closer prisoner than are his mistresses.

And now for a curious sight—the Cadi's divan, or Court of Justice, which may be seen on Thursdays in Tunis by the favoured few who succeed in gaining admittance, and which I will endeavour to describe here for the benefit of the many who fail in so doing. Picture to yourself a vast hall in the purest Arabian architecture, with stuccoed roof, fountained court, and frieze, over which precepts from the sacred Korán spread their graceful hieroglyphics. Up and down the pillared central space wander a busy, excited throng, who for the nonce have put off their usual Eastern impassivity. Beardless boys, aged men, and even some veiled women are there, the janissaries keeping the ranks, and all eyes fixed eagerly on the raised dais-room opening off the further end of the hall. Our guide pushes a way for us through the crowd, and a few whispered words to the janissaries procure us a foothold on the highest step of this sacred spot.

Here all is solemnity and silence, broken only by the voices of the pleaders and the accused. Round two sides of the room are ranged divans, and an empty throne between them represents the absent majesty of the Bey. Of the two divans, one answers to what in French law is termed the Cour de Cassation; the other is the Criminal Court. Four judges sit on the former, three on the latter. And well indeed do they fill their parts, if the majestic, grave benevolence and the awe-inspiring calm written on their grand countenances go for aught.

Seated cross-legged on the rich cushions of the divan, their heads are covered by turbans of a high shape peculiar to magnates of their calling; and round their shoulders are wrapped embroidered burnouses of the palest, most delicate dyes—the grey of the pigeon's breast, the green of spring's first leaf, the blushing pink of roses, the soft, tender blue of the sea; such colours and such tissues enfold them, as no common Arab could afford to drag through the soiling mire of the streets. Below these peep forth glimpses of the finest, whitest linen ever spun, and from their necks hang costly rosaries. The cadi himself, the most majestic of the seven, sits on the right-hand divan, a fair-skinned, grey-bearded patriarch. To my eye, accustomed to the swarthy Bedawys, with heads and legs turned copper-colour by the bronzing sun of Africa, the delicate skins, fair as a child's, of these men presented the most suggestive contrast, denoting as it does, the studious seclusion of their lives, the days and nights spent in pondering over the Korán and its code, a seclusion from which they never emerge, save to deal justice amongst the people out of the stored wisdom of their illuminated minds. What is finer than the face of one who has been accustomed to wield authority over the common herd? Decisions which none may question, glosses which none may contradict, pardon which no other dare bestow, doom which no other dare pronounce, the power which for years has been theirs alone, is stamped upon their thoughtful countenances; and this moral force is more potent to sway the masses who crouch at their feet than are all the swords of the janissaries who guard their portals.

As each case comes on the parties concerned in it, with those who plead for them, are ushered in, shuffling off their shoes as they gain the topmost step. At its conclusion they are cleared out by the guards to make way for new-comers. In the hall below the people wrangle and fight their quarrels over and over again; but such is the restraining power of that awful room that, as they enter, the words die on their lips, and they listen in deferential silence to the short sentences which proceed from those low-voiced, calm-eyed men.

A suit is just over between a man and the family of his divorced wife, whose separate estate he has failed to restore to them on ridding himself of her. The cadi pronounces the decree that restitution be made, as the law is when a wife is divorced for no fault of her own; and the crestfallen miser departs sullenly. And now a man who has been robbed bares his feet and enters to detail his wrongs. But the robber, where is he? The janissaries call his name aloud, it echoes through the long hall below; but he never appears, and the case is about to be adjourned till he can be produced, when a scuffle begins in the crowd without. A janissary has discovered the culprit, and is using force to bring him forward to the presence. He is a burly ruffian, and hits out right and left in his efforts to escape; but superior force prevails, and the panting wretch is at last hurled before his accuser. In their turn these two give way to a gentle, frightened girl, by name Habíba, who is not old enough to be veiled, but whose tender years have not prevented her from being abducted by a young ruffian. She had been tracked by her father and brought home, and is now here, under the escort of two black-veiled old women-relatives, to tell the tale of her wrongs. The cadi orders the offender to make amends by marrying her, and one can only hope that the child, who is but eleven years of age, will retain the affections of her boy-husband and lead a fairly happy life.

At last the hour of noon arrives; the court is rapidly cleared, and the cadi and his fellow-judges quit the divan, and, surrounded by their guards, pass down the steps and into the little mosque which opens by a door on the right from the main building. Their devotions concluded, they leave the mosque and pass slowly down the central hall; the people thronging to kiss the cadi's white bejewelled hand, which he extends to them benevolently. Arrived at the great door, they enter their closed carriages, lined with satin of yellow and other bright hues and drawn by four gaily harnessed black mules, and drive off to their houses followed by the admiring looks of the crowd. And so ends the cadi's weekly divan. But to me, left behind in the empty hall with my Moorish guide, a stranger sight than all presented itself.

In a stone cage—I can call it by no other name—built under an arch at the end of the court, raised about four feet from the level on which I stood, and fronted with thick iron bars, sat a wild beast, or rather a captive who resembled that more than anything else, with fettered legs, unkempt head, and haggard, staring eyes. He had committed a murder, and sentence of death was passed by the cadi upon him. But his family are trying to arrange for the *achat du sang*, and in the mean while, for a whole year, he has been kept chained up in that dark dungeon, with just light enough for the employment allotted him—that of making *checchias*, or fez caps. On Thursdays, when the court sits, he comes forward to peer through his bars at the crowd below; for might not his people be there with the ransom? The rest of the time he spends crouched in a corner, or bending over his work. Poor wretch! the months have passed by fruitlessly so far; and if they do not soon succeed in raising the money to redeem his life, he will one day be taken to the Bardo. Then the Bey will come from his summer palace at Marsa, and sit him down on the great throne that we wot of, with the black marble pillars on either side, and smoke his pipe, and silently pass his hand upwards over his moustache; and at that sign the doomed creature will be taken forth and despatched in the courtyard without. *La mort sans phrase*, indeed! He will go quietly enough; for is it not the will of Allah, Master of the worlds, and wherefore then should there be lamentations? Nay, better so, perhaps; for he might have been condemned to drag out life at the fetter's end in the Bagnio at La Goulette, where I have seen the poor rascals many a time toiling in the sun; and, as Thackeray has quaintly said, "I love not to think of thee with a chain at thy shin." Yes, better far than this is *la mort sans phrase*.

Envoi.

And so, at last, as all good things must end, the time came when we had to tear ourselves away from the White City, and this country of Mosques and Marabouts. Already the heat was getting unbearable, and there were rumours of an influx of the dreaded locusts; still, it was sadly that I bade farewell to the beautiful African shore as I watched it fading from the deck. Not long after, we found ourselves in Naples. I had imagined that at Naples fishermen lounged all day along the quays in red caps, dancing tarantellas, singing "Santa Lucia," and eating water-melons. I have spent six weeks there, and never once seen a red cap or heard "Santa Lucia," except from paid street bands. But Naples has been "improved." I am surprised that they have not improved away Vesuvius yet; but, no doubt, this will be arranged in time. Meanwhile they have done their best to conceal it by building nice, tall, new, white edifices everywhere, and you can drive quite a long way about the town without ever seeing it. I was told that they still wore the old Greek costume on the island of Procida. I went there. Every one walked about in ordinary dress. I tore my hair. I appealed to two *carabinieri* who were standing by. They said, after long reflection, that yes, there *was* one old woman who still had her dress. They took me to her (up three flights of stairs), and she produced it out of a cupboard. She put it on, stood up in it for about five minutes, and—charged me five francs for doing so! Alas! the waves of this nineteenth century, breaking across Europe, have washed over the sands of her picturesque past, and have reduced all lands and peoples to one dead level of civilized sameness. But the Moslem remains *tel quel*, and long may he so continue!

One day, in a restaurant at Naples, we tendered by mistake some Tunisian pennies. They could not, of course, be accepted; but a waiter, who had once been there, overhearing the conversation, came forward and offered to change them. His face lighted up as he inquired, "Monsieur et Madame viennent de Tunis?" Who knows? Perhaps he, too, had the nostalgia of the desert upon him. Perhaps he, like me, had felt the spell of that marvellous land. My fancy kindled, and for a moment I heard again the derboukas sounding, and saw the black musicians heating the parchment of them over the charcoal braziers; and once more I seemed, in imagination, to be gliding through the mysterious streets, and transported to the women's rooms, where the orange flowers smell sweet and the sequins shine, while the dance moves on voluptuously, and the moonlight floods the unroofed court.

I rejoice, O land of wonders, that my feet have trodden thy forests and thy cities. To thee, O beautiful, unforgotten Africa, greeting and farewell!

APPENDIX A.

(See page 54.)

The Ouled-Naïls.

"We must now mention a particular class of women, inhabitants of Biskra, who belong to the tribe of the Ouled-Naïl. They are one of the chief attractions of Biskra. Their complexions are very dark, of a reddish brown, and they darken them more, for they daub their faces with tar and saffron. They wear gaily coloured dresses, and an enormous amount of jewellery, of which they are very fond. Their hair is mixed with horsehair, and thick with grease and cosmetic; their raven tresses falling over the ears and enclosing their faces as if framed in ebony.... They dwell in a private quarter of Biskra, bearing their name, and dance in the Moorish cafés at night. They return, after a few years of this licentious living, to their native oasis, and almost invariably get married, their *fiancés* being more particular about the amount of cash forming their dowry than the morality of its source."—From *The Atlas* (a newspaper published in Algiers), February 27, 1893.

APPENDIX B.

(Page 79.)

The Difference between the Arabic of Literature and the Arabic of Modern Parlance.

A modern Arabic verb has but one form of conjugation and two tenses, the aorist (serving for present and future) and the preterit. There is no infinitive, but the 3rd pers. masc. sing. of the preterit serves as such, forming, as it does, the root. Example, *kteb* ("to write"), literally, "he has written." It has also the imperative mood, and the past and present participles. The "regular" Arabic verb, on the other hand, is conjugated with preterit, aorist indicative, aorist subjunctive, conditional, imperative, and what Professor Machuel describes as "*Aoriste Énergique Sourd*" and "*Aoriste Énergique Léger*," which answer to our "I will *certainly* kill," "Thou shalt *certainly* write;" in French, "*Certes, je tuerai*," etc.

The two following examples of the preterit of the verb "to kill" (*qt'l*) will show the difference between the "regular" and the spoken forms of Arabic :—

"Regular" Arabic.

Verb *to kill* (Qt'l).

PRÉTÉRIT.

Singulier.

1re personne		قتلت	qt'lt	*j'ai tué.*
2^e	,,	masc. }	qt'lt	*tu as tué.*
2^e	,,	fém. }	qt'lti	*tu as tué* (fém.).
3^e	,,	masc. }	qt'l (قتل, infinitive)	*il a tué.*
3^e	,,	fém. }	qt'let	*elle a tué.*

Duel.

2e personne			qt'ltma	*vous avez tué* (tous deux).
3^e	,,	masc. }	qt'la	*ils ont tué* (tous deux).
3^e	,,	fem. }	qt'lta	*elles ont tué* (toutes deux).

Pluriel.

1ʳᵉ personne			qt'lna	*nous avons tué.*
2ᵒ	,,	masc.	qt'ltoum	*vous avez tué.*
2ᵒ	,,	fém.	qt'ltoun	*vous avez tué* (fém.).
3ᵒ	,,	masc.	qt'lou	*ils ont tué.*
3ᵒ	,,	fém.	qt'lu	*elles ont tué.*

Modern or Spoken Arabic.

PRÉTÉRIT.

Singulier.

1ʳᵉ personne			qt'lt	*j'ai tué.*
2ᵒ	,,	masc.	qt'lt	*tu as tué.*
2ᵒ	,,	fém.	qt'lti	*tu as tué* (fém.).
3ᵒ	,,	masc.	qt'l	*il a tué.*
3ᵒ	,,	fém.	qt'let	*elle a tué.*

Duel.

(None.)

Pluriel.

1ʳᵉ personne			qt'lna	*nous avons tué.*
2ᵒ	,,	masc.	qt'ltou	*vous avez tué.*
2ᵒ		fém.	(None.)	
3ᵒ	,,	masc.	qt'lou	*ils (ou elles) ont tué.*
3ᵒ		fém.	(None.)	

I have given the French translation above, as the English "they" (unlike the French *ils* and *elles*) has no difference between singular and plural.

APPENDIX C.

(Page 130.)

Monsieur Charles Mismer gives the following account of the arrival of a party of French ministers and deputies who paid a visit of inspection to Algeria:—

"Tout mon temps se passait avec les Arabes . . . dans un café sur la place du Gouvernement. Un jour le canon retentit. En même temps, un vapeur pavoisé entra dans la rade. Il portait la fameuse caravane des ministres. Nous les vîmes défiler dans leurs equipages, au son de la *Marseillaise*, sous escorte de chasseurs d'Afrique.

"Sans se déranger, mes Arabes les contemplèrent d'un œil indéfinissable.

"Je plains ces hommes, dit l'un d'eux, on va les amuser avec des discours, des banquets, des représentations théâtrales; on leur montrera pêle-mêle des exploitations agricoles, des souvenirs archéologiques, des vignobles, des écoles, des champs d'alfa; on leur fera manger du *kouskous*, assaisonné de protestations de dévouement; finalement ils rentreront en France sans entrevoir le volcan qui bout sous leurs pieds."—"Souvenirs du Monde Musulman," par Ch. Mismer. Paris, 1892.

THE END.

www.ingramcontent.com/pod-product-compliance
Lightning Source LLC
Chambersburg PA
CBHW021846230426
43669CB00008B/1096